IRRESISTIBLE
Sound-Matching Sheets
and Lessons That Build
Phonemic Awareness

Quick Lessons, Word Lists, and Reproducible Sound-Matching Sheets That Use Favorite Children's Books to Reinforce Phonemic Awareness—and Delight Emergent Readers!

By Janiel Wagstaff

SCHOLASTIC
PROFESSIONAL BOOKS

New York ❖ Toronto ❖ London ❖ Auckland ❖ Sydney
Mexico City ❖ New Delhi ❖ Hong Kong ❖ Buenos Aires

Dedication

For all the dedicated teachers out there...a little time-saver!

Acknowledgments

Thanks to my family for supporting me through another writing project.

Thanks to all the authors and illustrators of the wonderful books included in this volume.
I love sharing them with kids!

Thanks to my supportive editors, Wendy Murray and Terry Cooper.

Thanks, too, Boo, for your humor and help with the word lists.

Cover design by Aartpack
Interior design by Grafica Inc.
Interior art by Maxie Chambliss
ISBN 0-439-16517-2

Copyright © 2001 by Janiel M. Wagstaff

Table of Contents

Letter to Colleagues 4

Introduction 5

CHAPTER 1:
Sound Boards:
Why, What, and How 9

CHAPTER 2:
Sound-Board Lessons:
Books, Boards,
Word Lists, Activities 19

Lilly's Purple Plastic Purse 21

*Animals Should Definitely
Not Wear Clothing* 27

Yoko 31

Jack's Garden 35

*Brown Bear, Brown Bear,
What Do You See* 39

The Snowy Day 42

Miss Nelson is Missing 46

*I Know an Old Lady
Who Swallowed a Fly* 50

The Wheels On the Bus 54

The Three Little Pigs 59

Where the Wild Things Are 64

The Paper Bag Princess 67

If You Give a Mouse a Cookie 72

Curious George Rides a Bike 76

Ten Black Dots 79

Mary Wore Her Red Dress 83

Corduroy 87

The Very Hungry Caterpillar 91

The Napping House 95

Who's in the Shed 100

Cookie's Week 104

Mrs. Wishy-Washy 108

*Five Little Monkeys
Jumping on the Bed* 112

Bread and Jam for Frances 116

CHAPTER 3:
More Sound-Board
Activities—and
Extensions 121

CHAPTER 4:
Sound Charts 137

References 144

Appendix A:
Phonemic Awareness
Background 145

Appendix B:
Levels of Phonemic
Awareness as described
by Adams 151

Phonemic Awareness
Assessments 151

Family Letter 155

Volunteer Instructions 156

Dear Colleague,

If you are a kindergarten or first-grade teacher, I'm sure you'll be pleased with how easy it is to incorporate phonemic awareness into your busy day using the great books you already enjoy and the sound boards included here. With this strategy you can integrate instruction and maximize time!

If you teach second grade, you can use the book, too. As a second-grade teacher myself, I've found that struggling readers and writers benefit from listening through words to match ending and vowel sounds. In fact, many state assessments include tasks that require students to do that very thing. Using the sound boards readies children for this type of activity.

The primary grades are full of children with varied phonemic awareness needs. The sound boards are so versatile that you can use them to accomplish different goals with different children!

What about teachers who work with older remedial students? You may have been looking for something to help your students develop critical phonemic awareness skills but have been disappointed that the activities you come across are geared for a young audience. Sound boards are the perfect solution! These gamelike activities are fun and appeal to older students as well as their younger counterparts.

Hope you enjoy using the sound boards. Happy teaching!

Janiel Wagstaff

P.S. You'll notice my publisher chose to call these activities sound-matching sheets in the title. My students and I like to call them sound boards—so that is how they are referenced in the book.

Introduction

Playing with sounds can be fun and easy. It's appropriate to introduce the idea of listening inside words early in children's development. Young children love to play sound games. They even do it spontaneously—playing with silly rhymes on the playground or walking home from school. Capitalizing on this natural interest in our classrooms fosters important skills—phonemic-awareness skills (Please note: if you are new to phonemic awareness, read Appendix A first.)

While on an airplane recently, I had an experience that reinforced how simple playing with sounds can be. A little girl (four years old, I found out later) was sitting with her mother, talking. As the plane took off, I heard her say, "Mom, let's play a game. I'll give you a word like *pot* and you give me a word like *hot*." Mom agreed and the girl gave her several words to rhyme. After a while she said, "Okay, Mom, now you give me some words." Her mother proceeded to say words for her daughter to rhyme. Then the girl said, "Ok, now let's change the game. I'll give you a word like *summer* and you give me a word like *sing*." She gave her mother several words and Mom responded with words that began with the same sound. Again, the girl later said, "Ok, now you give me some words." Mother and daughter played these word games for a while, laughing at some of their silly word suggestions. I laughed inside, too, thinking, *This kid could write a phonemic-awareness curriculum!* I try to encourage my students' parents to do similar things while waiting in line at the grocery store, driving in the car, sitting in the doctor's office, any spare moment.

Just as easily, you can use the sound boards and activities in this book to play sound games and make time for phonemic awareness in your students' day. But keep in mind that this is just one part of the literacy puzzle. While phonemic awareness and phonics are necessary for learning to read, they are not sufficient. Readers use many cues and employ multiple strategies as they construct meaning. Great teachers model and instruct students in all the skills good readers use. Phonemic awareness and phonics must take their place among the many components of a balanced literacy program. Balancing these components, like meeting the needs of all children, is a challenge teachers face every day.

How Phonemic Awareness Fits Into the Literacy Program

There is some disagreement over the proper use of phonemic-awareness research and its implications. Studies show that most students develop adequate phonemic-awareness skills by mid-first grade. Yet, some policy makers would mandate specific amounts of class time for phonemic-awareness training for all students (just as has happened with phonics) (Cole, 2000).

Some leaders in the field assert that specific attention to phonemic-awareness training benefits all preschool, kindergarten, and first-grade students by accelerating the rate of their reading and writing development (Adams et. al., 1998; Snow, Burns, & Griffin, 1998).

On the other hand, others, such as Regie Routman, argue that teachers have taught reading successfully for years without ever hearing the term *phonemic awareness* (2000).

...Research repeatedly demonstrates that, when steps are taken to ensure an adequate awareness of phonemes, the reading and spelling growth of the group as a whole is accelerated and the incidence of reading failure is diminished. These results have been obtained with normal as well as various at-risk populations.

Snow, Burns, & Griffin, 1998

Obviously, educators, both past and present, have used various strategies—including shared and guided reading and writing—to help students understand how word sounds work. Although it is possible to have a classroom of readers and writers who do not need phonemic-awareness practice, it seems that many students are coming to school without this skill. For example, I was recently teaching at-risk kindergartners in the Washington D.C. area and wanted to start their reading experiences with something familiar; I chose *Jack and Jill*. To my surprise, most of my students didn't know *Jack and Jill* or any other classical nursery rhymes. Not so surprisingly, most didn't understand the concept of rhyming words and had difficulty "hearing" rhyme. Assessments of these students showed that most of them needed help with phonemic awareness. Consequently, I integrated this instruction into our day and they all benefitted.

The percentage of students whose reading development is potentially at risk due to lack of phonemic awareness varies from source to source, as does the characterization of the problem's seriousness (Liberman, Shankweiler, & Liberman, 1991 as cited in Honig, 1996; Adams, 1990; Adams, et. al. 1998; Lyon, 1996, 1997; IRA, 1998; Cole, 2000; Routman, 2000). Certainly, those with more risk factors—little home-based literacy experience, low socioeconomic status, parents with histories of reading difficulty, language, cognitive, or certain health

Many times beginning readers struggle because they lack the thousands of hours of "prereading prerequisites" many of their peers have experienced. Phonemic awareness is the key...

Fitzpatrick, 1997

deficiencies—are more likely to need phonemic-awareness practice.

In designing the activities in this book, it was not my intention to participate in the debate or champion providing the same phonemic-awareness instruction for all students. Rather, I see this instruction as part of the broad repertoires of knowledge, skills, and resources teachers use as they respond to the needs of their students. I respect each teacher's judgement based on the needs of his or her students at any particular time and I lament any action (legislation, school board policy, or otherwise) that undermines professional autonomy.

What about the 20 percent of children who have not achieved phonemic awareness by the middle of first grade? The research on this is as clear as it is alarming. The likelihood of these students becoming successful readers is slim under current instructional plans.

International Reading Association Position Statement on Phonemic Awareness, 1998

As we incorporate phonemic-awareness activities into our instruction, it is essential to use common sense. We need to look at the needs of our current student population and keep our end goal in mind. Is it good use of time to use these activities with students who are already advanced as readers and writers? Remember, phonemic awareness is important because it facilitates reading and writing not as an end goal in itself. Understanding how sounds work in words and the ability to manipulate them allows children to respond more effectively to reading and writing instruction. If students are already there, give them more time to read and write!

Children who lack (phonemic awareness) should be helped to acquire (it); those who have grasped the alphabetic principle and can apply it productively should move on to more advanced learning opportunities.

Snow, Burns, & Griffin, 1998

Not long ago, at the end of a presentation in another school district, a kindergarten teacher told me that her school had just adopted a phonemic-awareness program for their kindergartners. Teachers had to teach only phonemic awareness for the first six months of the year. She shared, "You know it doesn't seem right. It's very hard to keep the kids from reading and writing." Surprised, I responded, "Keep the kids from reading and writing??!! We develop their phonemic awareness to facilitate reading and writing! If they want to read and write, by all means encourage them to do so!" Truly, phonemic awareness is best developed alongside reading and writing, not as a separate subject to be mastered. Any other approach certainly "doesn't seem right!"

Summing Up

We all know there is no one right way to teach reading and writing. There is no one cure-all for students who are having trouble. However, since phonemic awareness is so critical to reading and writing development, it is essential that teachers work diligently to support those students who lack it. The best approach is to integrate phonemic-awareness activities into meaningful literacy teaching. That's why the sound-board activities in this book are based on read-aloud and shared-reading experiences with great children's literature. The technique is so adaptable, it can be used with varied grouping arrangements and adjusted easily for difficulty and emphasis. Use the sound boards and other phonemic-awareness activities here to meet the varied needs of your students. View them as part of a balanced literacy program that ensures all students develop phonemic-awareness abilities and provides children who have deficits with supportive instruction. I hope you find great success and have fun, too!

Research indicates the most effective approach is a combination of direct sound-work activities and attention to print, including the learning of letter–sound correspondences.

IRA, 1998; Snow, Burns, & Griffin, 1998

The research findings related to phonemic awareness suggest that although (phonemic awareness) might be necessary it is certainly not sufficient for producing good readers. One thing is certain: We cannot give so much attention to phonemic awareness instruction that other important aspects of a balanced literacy curriculum are left out or abandoned.

International Reading Association Position Statement on Phonemic Awareness, 1998

SOUND-BOARD LESSONS:
Books, Boards, Word Lists, Activities

Straight Out of the Classroom

Thumbs Up, Thumbs Down is a favorite transitional activity I use with my kindergartners. They listen and repeat words I say, showing a "thumbs up" when the words begin with the same sound and a "thumbs down" when the words do not match. As each year begins, without fail I observe great insecurity as students look around the room at one another, change their minds and change their answers. I watch as thumbs down become thumbs up and thumbs up become thumbs down.

Many of my kindergartners are not accustomed to "listening inside words" (Fitzpatrick, 1997). They have been hearing language their whole lives, but have listened for meaning, not for sounds! Their insecurities remind me of the importance of phonemic-awareness practice. We can't just expect kids to "get it" on their own. Practice builds their abilities and confidence.

While walking down the first-grade hall, I observed a parent volunteer working with a boy. She had a list of simple three-letter words for him to read. They were on the word *pot*. The boy voiced each phoneme, "/p/, /o/, /t/." The parent replied, "Good. You know the sounds in the word! Now say them together." The boy repeated, "/p/, /o/, /t/." "Yes! You sounded it out! Now say it faster, put the sounds together." In frustration the boy repeated "/p/ /o/ /t/" again only at a faster rate of speed! He did not understand how to put the isolated sounds together into a meaningful unit.

How would this student ever learn to read without the ability to blend sounds together to make words?

During Writing Workshop one day in first grade, I modeled beginning a story about how my cats had fleas. Naturally, a few students also decided to begin writing about their pets. Kanisha called me over for help. She wanted to write about her cat. Our exchange went something like:

Ms. Wag: Great! What sounds do you hear in the word cat?

Kanisha: (replying with a confused look) Cat?

Ms. Wag: Yes. Say cat slowly. What sound do you hear at the beginning?

Kanisha: (repeating the word slowly) Cat?

Ms. Wag: Okay. Let's try to break the word apart. Like, /b/ is the first sound in bat, so what is the first sound in cat?

Kanisha: Cat?

Kanisha responded to several other prompts with the same answer and bewilderment. She obviously had a difficult time segmenting words into sounds or even understanding what I meant by my prompts.

How would Kanisha begin to represent words with letters without being able to "hear" the sounds? Often with children having difficulty like this, teachers segment the word slowly for them. But then, we are doing all the work. Phonemic-awareness activities allow students to practice and develop their abilities independently.

Deficiencies in phonemic awareness, the ability to work with sounds in words independent of letters and independent of meaning, can account for the difficulties experienced by the children in these vignettes. Students need to be able to hear, produce, and manipulate sounds in spoken words in order to blend words during reading and segment words during writing. Phonemic awareness, although studied for many years, has received great attention recently. Research has taught us that there are many students who do not develop phonemic awareness without instruction and that these children are at great risk of never becoming proficient readers and writers.

As I noticed my students having problems sounding and blending words, I wanted to address these problems in my teaching. However, it was only after extensive professional reading, combined with reflection on my teaching observations and practices, that I fully understood phonemic awareness and its importance. As I struggled to make time for phonemic awareness with my kindergartners, I developed the idea of **Sound Boards** to integrate these skills into my teaching. I use the **Sound-Board technique**, which includes the boards themselves along with activities based on accompanying word lists, to extend our daily read-aloud and shared-reading sessions.

Using this technique to experiment with words and sounds from our reading selections enables me to teach phonemic-awareness skills from a meaningful context without needing a lot of extra time. If you can relate to my "straight from the classroom" scenarios and want to combine phonemic awareness with shared reading and writing and ongoing demonstrations of how readers and writers work with words in a variety of contexts, try the sound-board activities in this book. (Twenty-four ready-to-use boards based on favorite children's books, word lists, and activities are included in Chapter 2.) To use the boards most productively and creatively, you need to understand phonemic awareness, how it relates to reading and writing development, and how it differs from phonics (See Appendix A for background information on phonemic awareness if you want to review before you begin.)

> *Children who lack phonemic awareness may have difficulties in sounding and blending new words, in retaining words from one encounter to the next, and in learning to spell.*
>
> *Snow, Burns, & Griffin, 1998*

What Are Sound Boards and How Are They Used?

Sound boards are simply sheets of paper that help you make a game of words and sounds. The paper is divided into four columns, with each column headed by a picture of an object or character associated with a book you and your students have read. For example for the book *Cookie's Week* by Cindy Ward and illustrated by Tomie dePaola, I drew simple pictures representing things in the story—Cookie, a toilet, a drawer, and some garbage. The sound board for *Mrs. Wishy-Washy* by Joy Cowley depicts the pig, the cow, Mrs. Wishy-Washy, and the duck.

Sound boards are used in a gamelike way to play with words and sounds. The technique makes practicing phonemic-awareness skills fun. Following a read-aloud or shared reading, each child in the group or class is given a copy of the related sound board. After identifying the pictures at the top of the columns, *you* set the focus by telling students to listen and match beginning sounds, ending sounds, or vowel sounds, for example. Each time you say a word that begins, ends, or echos the vowel of one of the column-header words, the students repeat it and try to match it with one of the column-header words— depending on your focus. For example, you might say *girl* and ask for a column-header word that begins with the same sound. The students should come up with *garbage*. When a match is made, students place a manipulative such as a unifix cube or coin, or an edible in the matching column.

Related sound board—one per child.

Cookie's Week: children's book read and enjoyed together.

During a lesson a teacher says aloud each character or object: Cookie, toilet, drawer, garbage/pig, cow, Mrs. Wishy-Washy, duck

Sound board for *Mrs. Wishy-Washy*.

You can model the correct answer for everyone to check. You may complete several examples before clearing the boards and putting them away for future use. Or you might clear the board and change the phonemic-awareness focus. "Now we'll listen to match rhyming words."

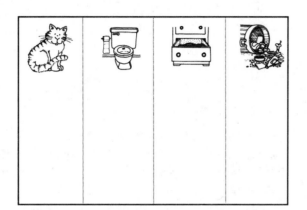

Cheerios™ are used to match beginning sounds: Table/toilet, candle/cookie, towel/toilet. Then more matches are made...

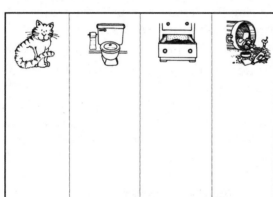

After students clear their boards, you might say: "Now let's listen for rhyming words. Rhyming words sound the same at the end like *bug* and *rug* and *four* and more. Your word to match is *floor*. Say *floor*. Now test it. Which word matches? Which word rhymes with *floor*? Put a Cheerio™ under the rhyming word."

What Skills Can I Teach and Reinforce with Sound Boards?

The word lists that accompany each sound board provide a number of possibilities for using each board to teach a range of phonemic-awareness skills. You might use the same board to work on rhyming with the whole class, matching beginning sounds with a small group, and matching ending sounds with an individual student. Be flexible. Every word list is not intended to be used with every book and every student. Rather, there will be plenty of opportunities to engage students in wordplay by reading multiple selections and using the sound boards in varied ways over time. Use the sound board only *after* you and your students have read and enjoyed its accompanying selection from a favorite chant, rhyme, or literature book.

The focus of the activities in this book is primarily on matching: matching rhyming words, matching the number of sounds in words (at the syllable and phoneme levels), matching beginning sounds (both single consonants and digraphs), matching ending sounds, and matching vowel sounds. However, a range of phonemic-awareness activities from simple to complex (Adams, 1990) follow each literature selection. You can also teach sound blending and segmenting with every sound board. (See pages 17-18)

Grouping

You can use sound boards to develop phonemic awareness with diverse groupings according to students' needs:

❖ **Whole class:** At the beginning of our kindergarten year, all of my students need to work on rhyming. I use sound boards with the whole group to follow up rich literature experiences with short wordplay sessions focused on hearing, matching, and providing rhyming words.

❖ **Small groups:** Research suggests that different children may need different amounts and forms of phonemic-awareness instruction and experiences (International Reading Association Position Statement on Phonemic Awareness, 1998). Once you have an idea of the skills your students need to strengthen, try smaller focus groups led by you, instructional aides, volunteers, or upper-grade students.

❖ **Individuals:** Students who are far behind or ahead of their peers will benefit from individual work. In addition to work in class with you, an aide, a volunteer, or an upper-grade student, ask parents or older siblings to get involved. Send the sound board, manipulatives, and word list or audiotape (explained in Chapter 3) home for extra practice or an extra challenge. (See Appendix B for examples of a letter to the family and instructions for volunteers.)

Use a favorite book character if you don't have a student whose name begins with a letter/sound you're working on.

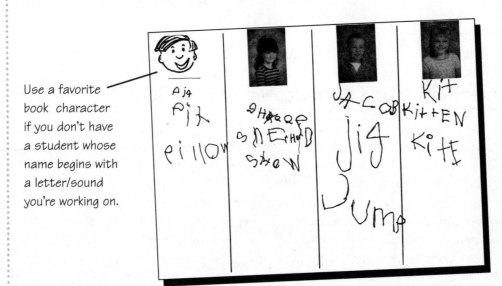

Jacob, a kindergartner completed this sound board at home by writing words with matching beginning sounds. See page 130 for more on class photo sound-matching.

Meeting Individual Needs

Students who are having difficulty matching sounds with a four-column board may find more success with fewer options. When preparing to work with such a group or individual, fold the board in half and photocopy only two columns. Or, fold back one column before copying to limit choices to three. If you are using previously copied boards, simply fold the extra columns under.

Adapted sound board for Mrs. Wishy-Washy.

Sample Lesson Sequence

❖ **Read:** Begin by enjoying the reading selection through reading aloud or shared reading. You may reread the book, rhyme, or chant multiple times, discuss the selection, act it out, and so on before using the sound board.

❖ **Introduce the sound board:** Have the children look at the sound board, pointing and identifying each column-header picture. Relate the pictures to the reading selection: "Who is pictured at the top of our sound board? Let's say their names as we point to them: pig, cow, Mrs. Wishy-Washy, and duck. Remember these are characters from the book *Mrs. Wishy-Washy.*"

❖ **Set phonemic awareness focus:** Explicitly tell children what they will be listening for (rhyming words, beginning sounds, and so on) and give a few examples: "Today we'll be listening for rhyming words. Rhyming words are words that sound the same at the end like *hit* and *spit*, *make* and *cake*, *hen*, and *pen*. Let's try to match some rhyming words with the characters at the top of your sound board."

❖ **Do an example together:** Model listening for the target sound and matching the sound to the board. Model testing the word to match with each picture on the board. Model marking the correct column of the board. Repeat the correct answer.

Teacher:	*Let's try one together. The word to match is luck. Say luck—l-uck*
Students:	*Luck.*
Teacher:	*Which word rhymes with luck? (wait time) Let's test each column. Say the words with me.*
Teacher and students:	*Pig—luck; cow—luck; Mrs. Wishy-Washy—luck; duck—luck.*
Teacher:	*Which word rhymes or sounds the same at the end as luck? Put a marker in the column of the word that rhymes with luck. (wait time). Say the rhyming word when you see five fingers. (Show one finger at a time until all five are extended.)*

Students:	Duck!
Teacher:	Yes, say duck and luck, duck—luck. Hear how these words rhyme. You should have a marker under duck because it rhymes with luck.

The Five-Finger Signal

This technique ensures that all children have "think" time and a chance to orally test columns before you give the answer. Tell students that you want them to take time to test the columns out loud but not give away the answer until you give them the signal by holding up one finger at a time, until all five are extended. Give the students wait time as you listen to them test columns. As their voices subside after testing the columns and all five of your fingers are up, everyone should respond with the answer and mark the appropriate column. When incorrect answers are given, model listening for the focus sound and testing the columns.

❖ **Continue testing and matching:** There are several examples in each word list. Don't feel obligated to use them all; they're merely suggestions. Keep the sound-board session short and fast paced. After students have time to test and match each word, model and repeat the correct answer.

Teacher:	Let's try another word. Match the word big. Say big—b-ig.
Students:	Big.
Teacher:	Which word rhymes with big? (wait time) Test each column.
Teacher & students:	Pig—big; cow—big; Mrs. Wishy-Washy—big; duck—big.
Teacher:	Which word rhymes with big? Put a marker in the column of the word that rhymes with big (wait time).
Students:	(When five fingers are extended) Pig!
Teacher:	Did you hear it? Pig and big rhyme. Say pig and big. Good! You should have one marker under duck and one marker under pig. Let's keep testing rhyming words…."

❖ **Sum up:** Repeat the phonemic-awareness focus of the lesson. Ask students to repeat any words they remember for the markers in each column. Example: "Today we worked on matching rhyming words. Remember, rhyming words are words that sound the same at the end. Who can remember some of the words we rhymed with *pig*? With *cow*? With *Mrs. Wishy-Washy*? With *duck*?"

Optional Activities

❖ **Non-examples:** Give some non-examples. "The word to match is *place*. Say *place—pl-ace*. Which word on our sound board rhymes with *place*? Test each word (wait time while students test words orally). You're right! I tried to stump you. There isn't a word on our board that rhymes with *place*!"

❖ **Volunteered words:** Ask students to volunteer their own words to match. "Who has a word that rhymes with one of the characters on our sound board? Your word must rhyme with *pig, cow, Mrs. Wishy-Washy,* or *duck.*"

Student:	Muck.
Teacher:	*Great. Everyone repeat the word.*
Students:	Muck.
Teacher:	*Now test the pictures. Which one rhymes with muck? Put a marker in the right column (wait time). Okay, everyone, which word rhymes with muck?*
Students:	Duck.
Teacher:	*You got it! Did you put your marker in the matching column?*

❖ **Test and match other volunteered words.**

Change of Focus: Change the phonemic-awareness focus of the sound board. If the session is moving along successfully and at a quick pace, simply have children clear all markers from their boards. Then, assign and model a new focus. Do an example or two, and continue to test and match. After working on rhyming words with *Mrs. Wishy-Washy*, for instance, use the board for work with beginning sounds. After your students have multiple experiences with sound boards and are becoming more phonemically aware, you can use the board for multiple foci during one session. I've frequently worked through rhyming words, beginning, and ending sounds in one session with kindergartners.

Sound Blending: Every board may be used to practice sound blending. When you introduce the board, or want to make a transition when you are changing the focus, tell students to match the word at the top of the page after blending the sounds you voice. "Blend these sounds and place a marker in the matching column. /P/ /i/ /g/ (wait time). What column did you mark? Why? Yes, the sounds /p/ /i/ /g/ blend together to make the word *pig*! Now, let's try another..." If students are having difficulty blending individual phonemes, voice larger word parts: the onset (sound that comes before the vowel), and the rime(s), (vowel(s) and consonants that follow it). "Blend these sounds and place a marker in the matching column. /P/ /ig/."

Sound Segmenting: Every board can also be used to practice sound segmenting. Ask students to match the number of sounds (phonemes) in new words to the column headers. To accomplish this, each word *must* be segmented and each sound counted. For example, *pig* has three sounds (/p/ /i/ /g/), so only other words with three sounds match (like: *bike* (/b/ /i/ /k/; *fox* (/f/ /o/ /x/).

Or, as a transition when changing the phonemic-awareness focus, have students segment just the column-header words. "Which of our words has four sounds? Put a marker under the picture (wait time). Yes, Yoko has four sounds, (model segmenting the word to hear each phoneme) /y/ /o/ /k/ /o/. Now, which word has five sounds? Say each word slowly, to hear every sound. Put a marker in the column under the word with five sounds (wait time). Yes, Valerie has five sounds. How do you know?" (Allow a student to segment). This is a way to practice sound segmenting to the phoneme level.

Points to remember

❖ ***Keep it fun and interactive!*** Don't do all the talking! Because phonemic awareness is the awareness of sounds in words, students should both hear and say the target words/sound often. Students should repeat words you say, orally segment words when they attempt to match sounds, and say each word in each column as they test the sounds. So, get your students talking!

❖ ***Model, model, model!*** As students develop phonemic awareness, your modeling is key. Model how to listen for the focus of the lesson. For example, if children are listening for beginning sounds, model segmenting and listening for that sound. "The word is *big*, /bbbbbb-ig/. If I say the word slowly, I can hear the beginning sound, /bbbbbb-ig/." Think aloud about how to match sounds using the board. "We're listening for and trying to match ending sounds. I need to say the word slowly and emphasize the last sound I hear. *Horse*, /hor-ssssss/. As I test the words in each column for a match, I need to say them slowly and emphasize their last sounds. /Hor-ssssss/—/shee-ppppp/. No, those don't match at the end."

Model, model, model! Attach a copy of the sound board to the board. It's easy to model matching sounds using magnets to mark the columns.

❖ ***Keep the pace quick:*** Students who need extra practice can work through the sound board again in small groups or independently, using a tape-recording of the session. The fast pace makes using the sound boards fun. See Chapter 3 for other phonemic-awareness activities and activities that extend the sound-board principles.

SOUND-BOARD LESSONS:

24 Books, Boards, Word Lists, Activities

This chapter includes sound boards for 24 familiar books to use for read-alouds and shared reading. Some selections have been published in Big Book format. This is noted for each book. If there is a Big Book, the ISBN is listed for both the regular and Big Book versions. Each sound board is accompanied by word lists for varied phonological awareness foci and additional sound-play activity ideas.

Sound-Board Column Setup

In some cases, fewer than four columns are needed to work with the sound board. For example, only two columns are needed when matching the number of syllables in column-header words for the book *Lilly's Purple Plastic Purse*. *Lilly* and *teacher* both have two syllables. *Purse* and *snack* both have one syllable. Students can fold under the two extra end columns (*snack* and *teacher*). If the order of the column-header words makes it impossible to fold the extra columns under, have students place a pencil or ruler in the unnecessary column(s) to remind them not to try to make matches there.

Using the Word Lists

Remember, the word lists represent a range of activities intended to meet different students' needs. It would be inappropriate to try to use all the lists for a literature selection in one sound-board session. Rather, choose lists based on students' current needs and keep the session short and fast paced. Change the focus only once or twice. Also, many more words are listed for each selection than should be used in a session, so you should not expect to use them all. Typically, students will have three or four markers per column per phonemic-awareness focus. That's already 16 words. Watch your students. If their attention wanes, the session may be too long or too difficult. You may need to stop and refocus or reduce the number of words to match. The purpose here is to provide you with options so you can meet your students' needs. Begin with the shorter words. They are easiest, since they have fewer sounds to hear and distinguish. As your students progress, use the longer, multisyllabic words.

When you're reading words from the lists, be sure to skip back and forth, from column to column randomly. This way students have to test the words to find appropriate matches. If you go down each column in order, all the words will match. Don't be afraid to try more difficult words even if your students may not be familiar with their meanings. If students are unaware of a given word, take a few minutes to explain. Vocabulary building is a side benefit of sound-board activities.

The word lists are provided for your convenience only. I often work with the boards without lists. Sometimes, though, I spend a little too much time between matches trying to think of words. Word lists can help keep up the pace, but you should feel free to work without them.

Lilly's Purple Plastic Purse
Author: Kevin Henkes
(1996) New York, NY: Greenwillow Books
ISBN: 0-688-12897-1

The Story

Lilly will amuse your students with the story of her new purple plastic purse, movie star glasses, and shiny quarters. She can't wait until sharing time to tell her classmates about her new possessions, and she ends up in trouble with her teacher, Mr. Slinger. All kids will relate to Lilly's frustrations and learn about problem solving from this adorable mouse's hilarious tale.

Using the Sound Board

The pictures represent **Lilly,** her **purse,** a **snack,** and her **teacher** (Mr. Slinger).

Word Lists

Use the following lists and the sound board to teach and reinforce phonemic awareness.

  Key:

  Italics: words directly from the book
  Regular font: other words

Match Rhyming Words

Lilly	purse	snack	teacher
hilly	curse	*pack*	feature
silly	verse	*back*	creature
Billy	nurse	*sack*	bleacher
Willy	worse	track	preacher
chili	rehearse	lack	
	reverse	Big Mac™	
	universe	attack	
		black	
		crack	
		plaque	
		shack	
		yak	
		haystack	
		racetrack	
		piggyback	
		jumping jack	

Match Number of Sounds (at the syllable level)

Lilly	**purse**
teacher	**snack**
(2 syllables)	**(1 syllable)**
pointy	milk
pencils	fish
Friday	desk
shiny	she
hallway	wore
rodents	sharp
around	go
glasses	set
tasty	new
curly	wrote
stories	star
surgeon	tune
movie	wait
morning	school
whisper	safe
recess	sad
quarter	thought
classroom	bag
bottom	small
crying	felt
awful	ran
cartoons	night
really	bake
plastic	note
disturb	props
happy	heart

Match Beginning Sounds

Lilly	**purse**	**snack**	**teacher**
lightbulb	plastic	sad	tie
lab	purple	Slinger	tasty
lunchroom	pointy	served	take
line	pencils	surgeon	toddler
lurched	privacy	sneaked	teenager
long	pupils	snapped	teeter-totter
last	picture	sampled	table
love	played	soul	toast
listen	props	skipped	toucan
look	peeked	circle	time
		student	test
		story	
		sunglasses	
		star	

Match Ending Sounds

Lilly	purse	snack	teacher
she	glass	chalk	her
shiny	class	stick	Chester
every	express	milk	Victor
privacy	bus	desk	father
be	furious	artistic	mother
cheesy	recess	neck	brother
tasty	face	week	answer
free		think	whisper
happy		look	entire
three		book	better
fiercely		bake	picture
really		take	
angry		think	
ready		peek	
story		back	
early			
sorry			
howdy			

Match Vowel Sounds

Lilly	purse	snack	teacher
/i/	/ur/	/a/	/ee/
clickety-click	purple	tack	she
fish	color	handle	greet
milk	circle	and	free
in	curl	had	movie
did	picture	Grammy	even
listen	furious	happy	creatively
picture	serve	hand	three
still	disturb	clap	week
big	mother	brand	erasers
simply	father	back	be
him	lurched	plastic	recess
little	picture	class	keep
with		bag	mean
		last	peek
		fat	

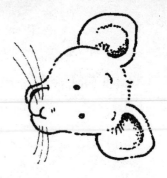

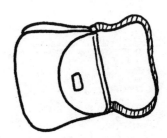

Other Phonemic-Awareness Activities
(with reading and writing extensions) for *Lilly's Purple Plastic Purse*

Sing a Song of Lilly (alliteration)

❖ Sing the song to the tune of *Mary Had a Little Lamb* as a class or with a small group. Record your singing for use in a listening center. Your song can follow this pattern:

> *Lilly loves her plastic purse*
> *Plastic purse*
> *Plastic purse*
>
> *Lilly loves her plastic purse*
> *Pretty and purple!*
> (repeats /l/ and /p/ words)
>
> *Lilly loves her pointy pencils*
> *Pointy pencils*
> *Pointy pencils*
>
> *Lilly loves her pointy pencils*
> *Pretty and pointy!*
> (repeats /l/ and /p/ words)
>
> *Lilly loves her goofy glasses*
> *Goofy glasses*
> *Goofy glasses*
> *Lilly loves her goofy glasses*
> *Gorgeous and glamorous!*
> (repeats /l/ and /g/ words)

❖ Innovate with students' names and possessions. For example:

> *Susana loves her shiny shoes*
> *Shiny shoes*
> *Shiny shoes*
> *Susana loves her shiny shoes*
> *Slick and super!*
> (repeat /s/ and /sh/ words)

❖ Extend this experience into shared and independent reading by writing song innovations on chart paper. Read and reread together, framing or highlighting /l/, /p/, /g/, or other words. Students can use fun pointers to reread the chart during Reading Workshop. You may also write a few verses on paper and give students copies for individual poetry/song folders.

Hammy Grammy Tongue Twisters (alliteration)

❖ Lilly goes shopping with her "Grammy" and returns to school with her purple plastic purse, movie star sunglasses, and three shiny quarters. Create your own tongue twisters about students' "Grammys." For example:

> *Brandon's Grammy buys balloons and bakes butter buns.*
> *Katie's Grammy keeps caterpillars in the kitchen.*

❖ Extend this activity by recording and illustrating the tongue twisters and binding them together into a Hammy Grammy Class Book. What a fun story to share with visitors if you have a "Grandparents Day"!

Sound Sort Center (sound matching)

❖ Cut the pictures from the top of the sound board. Sort objects into categories by matching their beginning sounds with the beginning sounds in the pictures (Lilly /l/, purse /p/, snack /s/, and teacher /t/). Have students bring small objects from home to add to the center, such as lightbulb, licorice, lace, leaf, leash; paperclip, pencil, toy plane, pea pod, plate, peanut; sock, seed, salt, sack, sand (in a small plastic bag), shell, ship, scissors; tack, top, toy, ticket, tinsel, toy tiger, tag, tea bag, tape

Also, put pictures of students whose names begin with /l/, /p/, /s/, and /t/ in the center.

For extra support, you might do this activity with the whole class or a small group before placing objects in the center.

❖ Students who are ready may record some of the /l/, /p/, /s/, and /t/ words in their personal dictionaries. (Names of the sorting center objects may be written on word cards and placed in the center for sorting.)

Other Reading/Writing Experiences
for *Lilly's Purple Plastic Purse*

Writing Notes

❖ Discuss how Lilly and her parents write notes to express their feelings to Mr. Slinger. Invite your students to write notes to you, the class, their parents, and each other. Model note writing by sharing a few notes you write to students. Ask students to read some notes to the class.

❖ On chart paper share and record purposes for note-writing. You might start your list by recording the purpose for writing a note in *Lilly's Purple Plastic Purse* (to express feelings, ask for forgiveness, and so on.)

Animals Should Definitely Not Wear Clothing
Author: Jan Barrett   Illustrator: Ron Barrett
(1970) New York, NY: Atheneum
ISBN: 0-689-20592-9
Big Book ISBN: 0-590-72616-1
(1991) New York: Scholastic

The Story
Your students will love the humorous text and illustrations as animals try on all sorts of crazy clothing. Each page demonstrates why animals should leave the dressing up to us.

The Sound Board
The pictures represent the **hen,** the **kangaroo,** the **giraffe,** and the **walrus.**

The Word Lists
Use the following lists and the sound board to teach and reinforce phonemic awareness.

Key:
Italics: words directly from the book
Regular font: other words

Match Rhyming Words

hen	kangaroo	giraffe	walrus
pen	Sue	staff	bus
wren	blue	laugh	fuss
then	flew	graph	Gus
Glen	glue	carafe	
pigpen	a-choo	paragraph	
playpen	accrue	half-and-half	
five-and-ten	shampoo		
	buckaroo		

Match Number of Sounds (at the syllable level)

hen	giraffe	kangaroo
(1 syllable)	**(2 syllables)**	**(3 syllables)**
should	**walrus**	*animals*
wear	*because*	*porcupine*
camel	*places*	*opossums*
wrong	*messy*	*terribly*

snake *silly* *embarrass*
lose *always* *disaster*
mouse *manage* *definite*
sheep *upside*
hot *mistake*
pig *clothing*
hard
life
goat
lunch
wet
moose

Match Beginning Sounds

hen	**kangaroo**	**giraffe**	**walrus**
hot	cat	jet	*wet*
hat	kiss	Jeff	*wear*
head	kite	jerk	west
hard	*could*	giant	when
handle	*camel*	jaguar	*would*
happen	*quite*	jealous	woman
handicap	kitten	Jessica	warrior
	carnival		wheelchair
	carnation		

Match Ending Sounds

hen	**kangaroo**	**giraffe**	**walrus**
in	do	if	sis
on	flu	off	bus
down	glue	*life*	fuss
sign	shoe	stuff	*mouse*
groan	threw	enough	*moose*
Nathan	mildew	photograph	*disastrous*
cyclone	shampoo	polygraph	fabulous
sharpen	bamboo		gorgeous
misshapen	interview		
fascination	brand-new		

Match Vowel Sounds

hen	kangaroo	giraffe	walrus
/e/	/a/	/ir/	/aw/
definitely	animals	never	drawn
get	camel	girl	hot
messy	manage	fur	not
wet	cantaloupe	spur	fought
letter	fantastic	pleasure	bought
fed	span	super	jot
sped	bland	bird	caught
bed	ran	squirting	
dressing	captain		
spend			

Other Phonemic-Awareness Activities
(with reading and writing extensions)
for *Animals Should Definitely Not Wear Clothing*

Animal Alliteration (alliteration)

❖ Challenge students to think of an animal and article of clothing beginning with the same sound. Examples: a snake in socks, a goat in glasses, a fox in a fur. After sharing, extend the alliteration into full sentences or phrases like those in the book. Animals should definitely not wear clothing...*because a snake in socks would look silly, because a goat in glasses would be goofy, because a fox in a fur would look funny.*

❖ Use these funny alliterations to write and illustrate your own class book.

Create A Rhyme (rhyming) (Blevins, 1998)

❖ Have students fill in the missing word with a rhyming article of clothing.

Once I Saw

Once I saw a cat,
And it wore a funny little _____.
Tra-la-la, la-la-la-la-la-la
Silly little cat.

Once I saw a mouse,
And it wore a funny little_____.
Tra-la-la, la-la-la-la-la-la
Silly little mouse.

Words for Poem	
cat—hat	mouse—blouse
goat—coat	newt—suit
fox—socks	kittens—mittens

Yoko

Author: Rosemary Wells
(1998) New York: Scholastic
ISBN: 0-439-10472-6

The Story

Poor Yoko! Everyone in class makes fun of her favorite foods. Students will empathize with Yoko's plight while learning about different cultural cuisines, tolerance, risk-taking, and friendship.

The Sound Board

The pictures represent **Yoko, sushi, Frank,** and **Valerie.**

The Word Lists

Use the following lists and the sound board to teach and reinforce phonemic awareness.

> Key:
> *Italics: words directly from the book*
> Regular font: other words

Match Rhyming Words

Yoko	sushi	Frank	Valerie
cocoa	loosely	rank	gallery
loco	pushy	bank	salary
	woodsy	stank	
		blank	

Match Number of Sounds (at the syllable level)

Frank (1 syllable)	Yoko, sushi (2 syllables)	Valerie (3 syllables)
lunch	*today*	*favorite*
rice	*cheery*	*wonderful*
school	*blossom*	*everyone*
friends	*mother*	*Timothy*
class	*cooler*	*cucumber*
nuts	*meatball*	*coconut*
beans	*sandwich*	*spaghetti*
stew	*seaweed*	
	cooking	
	tuna	

Match Beginning Sounds

Yoko	sushi	Frank	Valerie
you	*soup*	*for*	vine
yuck	*song*	*food*	vote
yard	*stew*	*fish*	vest
yank	*smoothie*	*Fritz*	*very*
yo-yo	*sandwich*	*friendly*	valentine
yesterday	*suddenly*	*forget*	
		favorite	

Match Ending Sounds

Yoko	sushi	Frank
no	**Valerie**	ick
blow	*Jelly*	*yuck*
hello	*very*	*snack*
mango	*tree*	track
willow	*cheery*	*shark*
arrow	*honey*	*attack*
follow	*hungry*	*pancake*
	smoothie	*clickety-click*
	Timothy	
	everybody	
	spaghetti	

Match Vowel Sounds

Yoko	sushi	Frank	Valerie
/o/	**/u/**	**/a/**	**/a/**
go	noon	day	mat
show	*blew*	sang	*crab*
cones	stew	rang	*snack*
whole	cooler	late	*packed*
opened	*Tulip*	made	*salad*
willow	*smoothie*	*Hazel*	*sandwich*
mango		*favorite*	*bamboo*
potato			
coconut			

Other Phonemic-Awareness Activities
(with reading and writing extensions) for *Yoko*

Guess our Favorite Foods (sound blending, sound matching)

❖ Play a guessing game focusing on one of everybody's favorite subjects: food. Model how to play by thinking of a favorite food and giving hints by voicing sounds in order. For example, "I'm thinking of a favorite food. It begins with /p/." Students say the sound and try to guess (could be *pie, pizza, peas, prawns, popcorn, peanuts,* or *portobello mushrooms*). Then voice the next sound, syllable, or chunk in turn, each time allowing guesses. "/i/" (could be *peas, pizza, peanuts*) "/z/"... "/a/" Play as a class or in groups.

❖ Illustrate food favorites, sort them for sounds in centers, then bind them into a class book.

Favorite Food Tunes (sound manipulation, rhyming)

Favorite food
Favorite food
Playing with my favorite food
Pizza, lizza, gizza, mizza,
Favorite, favorite food!

With this activity, it's okay to play with your food. Create your own silly food tunes. Take a favorite food, segment off the beginning phoneme, add another, blend...and you have a silly rhyming tune.

Variation on Favorite Food Tunes (alliteration, sound matching)

Favorite foods
Favorite foods
These are all my favorite foods
Pizza, popcorn, pineapple, pie
Favorite, favorite foods!

Instead of singing rhyming foods, think of foods beginning with the same sound. Another variation is to sing foods with the same ending sound. You can write any of the favorite food tunes on shared-reading posters for reading and rereading (the kids love them!) or publish on classroom walls or in a class book.

Jack's Garden
Author: Henry Cole
(1995) New York: Greenwillow Books
ISBN: 0-688-13501-3

The Story

Jack's Garden is one of my favorite springtime books to launch the planting of our own class garden. Henry Cole uses cumulative text structure, based on the classic *The House That Jack Built,* to illustrate the changes and growth of Jack's beautiful garden. The page borders stimulate scientific inquiry with their detailed illustrations and labels.

The Sound Board

The pictures represent ***seeds, Jack, rain,*** and ***sprout.***

The Word Lists

Use the following lists and the sound board to teach and reinforce phonemic awareness.

Key:

Italics: words directly from the book

Regular font: other words

Match Rhyming Words

seeds	Jack	rain	sprout
weed	tack	mane	pout
feed	sack	lane	shout
bleed	rack	brain	sprout
speed	black	grain	about
indeed	Big Mac™	Spain	sauerkraut
exceed	attack	complain	
centipede	haystack		
millipede			

Match Beginning Sounds

seeds	Jack	rain
sprout	Joe	row
so	*June*	ride
soil	giant	*rake*
stem	gentle	*roots*
slug		

snake
spider
sipped
spotted
stinkbug
swallow
sunflowers

jealous
juniper
January

roach
robin
rooster
raspberry

Match Ending Sounds

seed	**Jack**	**rain**	**sprout**
bud	rake	on	wet
bird	pink	can	that
cloud	hollyhock	June	spot
planted	pitchfork	brown	root
buried		robin	plant
blossomed		garden	adult
centipede		grapevine	insect
			spiderwort

Match Vowel Sounds

seed	**Jack**	**rain**	**sprout**
/ee/	**/a/**	**/a/**	**/ou/**
bee	cat	lace	our
flea	ash	made	sour
weed	that	gray	brown
leaf	plant	snake	cloud
green	black	daisy	trowel
beetle	aster	chased	ground
seedlings	admiral	ladybug	flowers
centipede		grapevine	

Other Phonemic-Awareness Activities
(with reading and writing extensions) for *Jack's Garden*

Garden Sorting (sound matching)

❖ Every spring, no matter what grade I am teaching, my students and I plant a garden. I've used *Jack's Garden* to stimulate inquiry about materials needed to start and maintain the garden. As we gather these materials, we label them and sort them for sounds. For example, *shovel* matches *shears,* and *soil* matches *seeds,* and so on. As we gather seed packs, we sort those, too. As we plant seeds, we label each area using interactive writing. Copies of the labels are placed in a center for sorting. As the garden grows and changes, we record our observations in learning logs, in words and pictures.

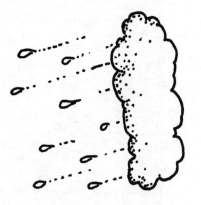

Brown Bear, Brown Bear, What Do You See?
Author: Bill Martin, Jr.   Illustrator: Eric Carle
(1983) New York: Henry Holt and Co.
ISBN: 0-8050-0201-4

The Story

Every early childhood teacher reads this classic. It's great for practicing color words and playing with the repetitive, patterned text.

The Sound Board

The pictures represent the **bear,** the **sheep,** the **fish,** and the **mother.**

The Word Lists

Use the following lists and the sound board to teach and reinforce phonemic awareness.

Key:
Italics: words directly from the book
Regular font: other words

Match Rhyming Words

bear	sheep	fish	mother
tear	keep	wish	brother
Blair	deep	dish	smother
scare	sweep	swish	
lair	cheap	anguish	
flair	Jeep™	establish	
stair	peep	embellish	
	creep		

Match Number of Sounds (at the syllable level)

bear	mother
sheep	**(2 syllables)**
fish	*redbird*
(1 syllable)	*looking*
what	*yellow*
do	*purple*
you	*goldfish*
see	*children*
at	
me	
duck	
blue	
horse	
green	

frog
cat
white
dog

Match Beginning Sounds

bear	sheep	fish	mother
bird	she	*frog*	me
blue	sheet	flea	Mr.
black	shovel	fork	motor
beautiful	shower	fumble	mango
brown	showcase	favorite	mailbox
	shape	fabulous	microphone
	shine	far	mischief
	shadow		master
			marble
			marker

Match Ending Sounds

bear	sheep	fish	mother
rare	dip	wash	sister
fare	flip	rush	liver
pear	ketchup	Welsh	bother
chair	deep	dish	wonder
affair	checkup	bash	blender
snare	slope	mush	straighter
snore	cantaloupe	blush	
fur		bush	
jar		push	

Match Vowel Sounds

bear	sheep	fish	mother
/air/	**/ee/**	**/i/**	**/er/**
chair	*green*	*children*	*bird*
dare	*we*	bit	*purple*
there	*see*	win	term
pear	bleed	fridge	learn
	read	Smith	purpose
	feed	missing	journey
	screen	intake	runner
	centipede	village	word
	emergency	quiver	earning
	catastrophe		
	detective		

The Snowy Day
Author: Ezra Jack Keats
(1981) New York, NY: Viking Press

ISBN: 0-104-050182-7

The Story

The Snowy Day is another classic every teacher reads. I like to read it on the first snow day of the season. Just as Peter enjoys experimenting with snowballs, snow angels, and the like, we brainstorm all the fun activities we may enjoy in the snow. This year, I took pictures of the students playing in the snow, making a snowman, writing their names in the snow, making tracks, etc. We recorded text with interactive writing and bound the pages together into a class Big Book titled: *Our Snowy Day.*

The Sound Board

The pictures represent **Peter,** his **snowsuit,** the **stick,** and the **angel.**

The Word Lists

Use the following lists and the sound board to teach and reinforce phonemic awareness.

    Key:

Italics: words directly from the book

Regular font: other words

Match Rhyming Words

Peter	snowsuit	stick	angel
eater	root	*pick*	well
heater	shoot	brick	fell
feeder	flute	lick	spell
two-seater	execute	flick	swell
	pollute	chick	tell

Match Number of Sounds (at the syllable level)

stick	Peter
(1 syllable)	snowsuit
woke	**angel**
night	**(2 syllables)**
snow	*outside*
path	*morning*
street	*piled*
crunch	*pointing*
	slowly
	something

sank   sticking
toes   mountain
tracks   mother
slid   snowball
    pocket

Match Beginning Sounds

Peter	snowsuit	angel
put	stick	a
piled	see	ape
path	street	ace
pointing	sank	acorn
plop	something	Asia
pretended	smacking	able
picked	so	aide
packed	smiling	
pocket	slid	
	sad	
	sun	
	still	

Match Ending Sounds

Peter	snowsuit	stick	angel
winter	out	track	all
after	night	woke	smile
climber	put	make	hall
another	street	sank	fall
mother	feet	like	pile
adventure	that	walk	fell
together	thought	smack	snowball
	fight	took	tall
	wasn't	sock	handful
	yet		still
	pocket		
	about		
	wet		
	slept		
	breakfast		

Match Vowel Sounds

Peter	snowsuit	stick	angel
/ee/	/o/	/i/	/a/
he	woke	winter	make

see	*window*	*it*	sank
street	*toes*	*his*	and
feet	*slowly*	*this*	made
tree	*old*	*in*	great
be	*so*	*big*	Blake
pretended	*blowing*	*slid*	mistake
heaping	soldier	*into*	
before		*still*	
dream			
deep			

Other Phonemic-Awareness Activities for *The Snowy Day*

Tap Those Sounds (sound segmentation)

❖ Peter uses a stick to make tracks and tap the snow out of a tree in *The Snowy Day*. Give students rhythm sticks to tap out the sounds in words. They can tap two sticks together or tap one on a table or desk. Use words from the book and instruct students to tap and say each sound in the word. "When Peter comes in from his adventures outside in the snow, he takes a warm bath in the tub. Tap and say the sounds in *tub*. /t/ /u/ /b/." If students are having difficulty, practice tapping onset and rime before tapping phonemes. Don't forget to model, model, model.

This is a fun activity to record and send home with students who need more help. Send home the tape with a pair of rhythm sticks.

Other Phonemic-Awareness Activities
for *Brown Bear, Brown Bear, What Do You See?*

Animal Search (sound blending, sound matching)

❖ Hide plastic animals around the room. Give students sound clues to identify the animals and where they are hidden. Use the text pattern. "Students, students what do you hear? /p/ /i/ /g/." After students guess the animal, continue with, "Pig, pig where are you hidden? /b/ /ook/ /c/ /ase/." When the location is guessed, send a volunteer to find the plastic animal. Play as a class or in groups. Place plastic animals in a sound sorting center. Students can sort for beginning sounds, ending sounds, rhyming words, and so on.

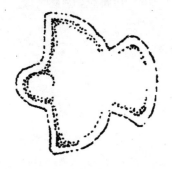

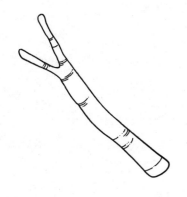

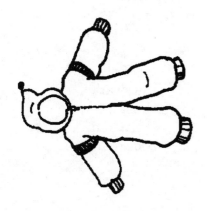

Miss Nelson Is Missing!

Authors: Harry Allard and James Marshall
(1977) Boston: Houghton Mifflin Co.
ISBN: 0-395-25296-2

The Story

All students benefit from the lesson Miss Nelson's kids learn when she turns up missing. Having the mean and horrible substitute, Miss Viola Swamp, teaches the children to appreciate their teacher.

The Sound Board

The pictures represent **Miss Nelson, Viola Swamp, homework,** and a **shark.**

The Word Lists

Use the following lists and the sound board to teach and reinforce phonemic awareness.

> Key:
> *Italics: words directly from the book*
> Regular font: other words

Match Rhyming Words

Nelson	Viola	homework	shark
fun	cola	jerk	ark
bun	victrola	perk	bark
gun	crayola	quirk	dark
done		smirk	spark
sun		berserk	aardvark
		clockwork	ballpark
		teamwork	monarch
			bookmark

Match Number of Sounds (at the syllable level)

shark (1 syllable)	Nelson homework (2 syllables)	Viola (3 syllables)
Miss	*missing*	*terrible*
kids	*spitballs*	*unpleasant*
school	*settle*	*history*
squirm	*giggled*	*misbehave*
rude	*refused*	*perfectly*
Swamp	*teacher*	*detective*
witch	*snapped*	*butterflies*
house		*discouraged*

Mars	business	forever
swarm	story	certainly
hall	police	
song	wicked	
	gobbled	
	footsteps	
	secret	

Match Beginning Sounds

Nelson	Viola	homework	shark
now	voice	whole	she
not	very	have	shut
next	violin	hard	should
new	vein	help	shades
never	vacation	house	shine
noticed	vegetable	happened	shout
nice		hall	shrink
nature		here	shingle
nocturnal		hello	shoulder
		hung	

Match Ending Sounds

Nelson	Viola	homework	
in	cola	**shark**	
down	Motorola™	make	
even	chinchilla	black	
done	victrola	stuck	
can		desk	
plane		arithmetic	
woman		book	
assign		work	
listen		think	
chin		ask	
drawn			
happen			
children			

Match Vowel Sounds

Nelson	Viola	homework	shark
/e/ as in egg	**/i/**	**/o/**	**/ar/**
settle	right	loaded	sorry
lessons	sign	no	hard
next	find	hello	Mars

47

yelled	*assigned*	*"oh"*	*car*
dress	*tightly*	*noticed*	art
desk	*likely*	*home*	smart
never	*flies*		Kmart™
went	*cried*		aardvark
them	*smile*		sweetheart
help			
exclaimed			
steps			
tell			

Other Phonemic-Awareness Activities
for *Miss Nelson Is Missing*

What Sound Is Missing? (sound segmentation)

❖ Challenge students to locate missing sounds from words in *Miss Nelson is Missing*. Say words from the book, deleting chunks, beginning, middle, or ending sounds. Students have to find the missing sound to figure out each word. Teacher: "I'll say a word from the story with a missing sound. You try to figure out the word. /Shar/." Students: "Shark!" Teacher: "Great! What sound was missing? "Students: /k/." Teacher: "Where did it belong?" Students: "At the end."

I Know An Old Lady Who Swallowed a Fly
Author: Rose Bone   Illustrator: Alan Mills
(1961) Rand McNally & Co.

The Story

A favorite to sing and a favorite to read. Look for varied versions of *I Know An Old Lady* and share them with your class. Then have the students make comparisons. Examples of variations include: *I Know an Old Lady Who Swallowed a Fly* retold by Nadine Bernard Westcott (1980), Boston: Little, Brown and Company; and *I Know an Old Lady Who Swallowed a Pie* by Alison Jackson (1997), New York: Dutton Children's Books.

The Sound Board

The pictures represent the **bird,** the **dog,** the **goat,** and the **horse.**

The Word Lists

Use the following lists and the sound board to teach and reinforce phonemic awareness.

> Key:
> *Italics: words directly from the book*
> Regular font: other words

Match Rhyming Words

bird	**dog**	**goat**	**horse**
absurd	*hog*	*throat*	*course*
blurred	clog	boat	force
heard	fog	coat	source
purred	jog	float	air force
slurred	log	note	resource
spurred	bullfrog	mote	reinforce
stirred	groundhog	wrote	remorse
third	catalog	vote	
word		remote	
absurd		raincoat	
backward			
crossword			
overheard			

Match Beginning Sounds

bird	**dog**	**goat**	**horse**
bet	*don't*	*guess*	*her*
bite	*die*	go	*how*
big	*dead*	gold	*hog*
best	dine	gotcha	hamper
burger	dinner	gamble	headache
balance	disaster	gorgeous	hilarious
because			

Match Ending Sounds

bird	**dog**	**goat**	**horse**
old	*hog*	*that*	*guess*
swallowed	big	*but*	*course*
inside	long	*cat*	mess
wriggled	gag	*just*	less
tickled	sag	*what*	confess
bed	swig	*walked*	lots
glad	chug	popped	spoons
afraid	ladybug		glass
weird			dismiss
homemade			

Match Vowel Sounds

bird	**dog**	**goat**	**horse**
/ir/	**/o/**	**/o/**	**/or/**
spider	*hog*	*swallow*	*course*
her	hot	old	more
stir	stop	*opened*	floor
blur	operate	*throat*	bore
fur	yawn	*know*	store
rumor	cough	*don't*	performer
pleasure	awful	crow	order
	autumn	blow	explored
		leftovers	scorch
		sideshow	floral
		overflow	

Other Phonemic-Awareness Activities
for *I Know An Old Lady Who Swallowed a Fly*

I Know A Sound (sound matching)

❖ Adapt the "Old Lady" chant to play sound matching. Voice a beginning sound and repeat the chant below. At the end, children call out as many matching words as they can. Or, you may quickly point to volunteers.

I know a word that starts with /h/
Say it with me: /h/, /h/, /h/
Perhaps it's _____.

❖ Adapt the chant in multiple ways:

I know a word that rhymes with / /...
I know a word that ends with / /...

This is a fun activity to record and place in a listening center. Children enjoy coming up with additional matching words and revel in trying to hear themselves offering matching words in the recording.

The Wheels on the Bus

Adaptor and Illustrator: Paul O. Zelinsky
(1990 & 2000) New York: Dutton Children's Books
ISBN: 0-525-44644-3
Big Book ISBN: 0-440-84677-3
Adapted by Maryann Kovalski
(1987) Trumpet Club

The Story

This pop-up version really gets kids motivated to read and reread. Try the Big Book version and the innovation called *The Seals on the Bus* by Lenny Hort (2000), Henry Holt & Co.

The Sound Board

The pictures represent movement from the book: ***round and round, open and shut, move on back,*** and ***up and down.***

The Word Lists

Use the following lists and the sound board to teach and reinforce phonemic awareness.

Key:
Italics: words directly from the book
Regular font: other words

Match Rhyming Words

(round and)	(open and)	(move on)	(up and)
round	**shut**	**back**	**down**
around	cut	pack	*town*
hound	but	rack	frown
frowned	mutt	track	brown
clowned	glut	Big Mac™	drown
ground	what	attack	ball gown
sound	chestnut	black	crosstown
campground	haircut	crack	renown
greyhound	coconut	plaque	out-of-town
playground	halibut	piggyback	
year-round		jumping jack	
merry-go-round			

Match Beginning Sounds

(round and)	(open and)	(move on)	(up and)
round	**shut**	**back**	**down**
riders	*shh!*	*bus*	*doors*
rail	shove	*bumpity-bump*	damp
road	shoes	*babies*	dig
radio	shine	baaah!	dinner
ringer	shoulder	beat	disabled
roll	shape	balance	dinette
rest	sharpener	buttercup	ditch
racoon	shoot	battleship	different
ramble	shag	Band-Aid™	dandelion
ranger	shawl	bragger	diver
rooster		boots	Danish
wrap		burner	deliver
		bottle	

Match Ending Sounds

(round and)	(open and)	(move on)	(up and)
round	**shut**	**back**	**down**
ride	*out*	look	*on*
slide	wait	sick	*town*
bad	left	think	*open*
tried	crust	neck	*in*
made	spent	peek	spoon
good	popped	slick	drawn
blood	forgot	spoke	crayon
lemonade	wrapped	fake	entertain
	bandit		

Match Vowel Sounds

(round and)	(open and)	(move on)
round	**shut**	**back**
down	**/u/**	**/a/**
/ow/	*bus*	*waaah!*
town	*bump*	tack
out	*mothers*	handle
bounce	putter	hammer
frown	flutter	band
outrage	stumble	plastic
howl	wonder	class
gown	junkyard	shadow
mound	color	branded
sound	suddenly	black

Other Phonemic-Awareness Activities
for *The Wheels on the Bus*

Sing the Sounds in the Word (sound blending) (Fitzpatrick, 1997)

❖ Use the tune of Wheels on the Bus to practice blending sounds.

The sounds in the word go /b/ /u/ /s/, /b/ /u/ /s/, /b/ /u/ /s/,
The sounds in the word go /b/ /u/ /s/,
Can you guess the word?

Sing What They Say (sound matching)

❖ The characters from *The Wheels on the Bus* can only say syllables that begin with the same sound as their names. Sing what they may say to the tune of "The Wheels on the Bus." For example,

The driver on the bus says do, dee, dah; do, dee, dah; do, dee, dah
The driver on the bus says: do, dee, dah
All through the town.

The babies on the bus say boo, bee, baa; boo, bee, baa; boo, bee, baa
The babies on the bus say boo, bee, baa
All through the town.

Other possible characters to sing about: people, riders, mommies, daddies, ladies, men, children, boys, girls, animals, and so on.

Variations: (sound matching)

❖ Have the characters only say *words* that begin with the same sound as their names.

The driver on the bus says: diaper, doughnut, door; diaper, doughnut, door;
diaper, doughnut, door.
The driver on the bus says: diaper, doughnut, door
All through the town.

❖ Leave out the identity of the characters. Students must use first sounds as clues to whom the mystery person is.

These people on the bus say: milk, move, may; milk, move, may; milk,
move, may.
These people on the bus say: milk, move, may
Who are they? (Mommies)

The Seals on the Bus by Lenny Hort (2000), Henry Holt & Co. (rhyming)

❖ *The Seals on the Bus* is a great example of the fun innovations you can create with familiar rhymes and tunes. Kids will love this silly book and its funny illustrations. Challenge your students to follow the pattern of *The Seals on the Bus*, which substitutes rhyming words for words in *The Wheels on the Bus*. Examples from *Seals* are: *seals* for *wheels* and *vipers* for *wipers*.

Can you substitute rhyming words for:

The *doors* on the bus...(example: *boars*)
The *headlights* on the bus...(*mites*...go *bite, bite, bite*)
The *chairs* on the bus...(*bears*...go *growl, growl, growl*)
The *brakes* on the bus...(*snakes*...go *hiss, hiss, hiss*)
The *gears* on the bus...(*deer*...go *prance, prance, prance*)
The *riders* on the bus...(*spiders*...go *weave, weave, weave*)

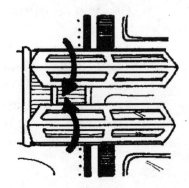

The Three Little Pigs
Author: James Marshall
(1989) E P Dutton
ISBN: 0-803-70591-3

The Story
This classic tale comes in so many versions. James Marshall's is one of my favorites. Compare the different ways the versions end. Act them out.

The Sound Board
The pictures represent the **pig,** the **wolf,** the **straw,** and the **bricks.**

The Word Lists
Use the following lists and the sound board to teach and reinforce phonemic awareness.

Key:

Italics: words directly from the book

Regular font: other words

Match Rhyming Words

pig	wolf	straw	bricks
big		ma	*sticks*
wig		pa	*six*
dig		law	*picks*
rig		hee-haw	tricks
swig		raw	wicks
twig		flaw	licks
bigwig		coleslaw	mix
thingamajig			fix
			kicks
			fiddlesticks
			pick-up-sticks

Match Beginning Sounds

pig	wolf	straw	bricks
puffed	*world*	sow	*be*
pooh	*which*	sent	*build*
pretty	*would*	seek	*business*
pick	*work*	said	*building*
put	*well*	set	*blow*
park	*worth*	so	*blew*
plaster	*we*	second	*bought*

59

popcorn	*when*	*sticks*	*bit*
poster	*went*	*sooner*	*busy*
people	*why*	*settled*	*basketful*
pea	*well*	*still*	*back*
parachute	*way*	*sturdy*	*boiling*
pilot	wicked	*solid*	*butter*
pineapple	wonderful	*stood*	
	wasteful	*smile*	
	wheelbarrow	*scrumptious*	
		six	
		sorry	

Match Ending Sounds

pig	**wolf**	**straw**	**bricks**
morning	*huff*	*ha*	*once*
boiling	*puff*	*saw*	*that's*
approaching	*off*	gnaw	*business*
hog	*enough*	flaw	*house*
big	tough	seesaw	*ourselves*
gag	slough	blah	*let's*
wag	stuff	spa	*turnips*
flog	triumph	la-di-da	*this*
bug	scuff		glass
chug	Jeff		space
slug	Vanderhoff		express
talking			place
egg			
swig			
underdog			
tagalong			
tiptoeing			

Match Vowel Sounds

pig	**wolf**	**straw**
/i/	**/oo/**	**/aw/**
bricks	*good*	*all*
little	*would*	*saw*
into	*put*	*bought*
which	*could*	ball
chin	*cooked*	stalk
this	foot	taught
sticks	wood	long
it	*should*	install

pretty
still
didn't
bricks
bit
solid
pick
six
turnip
splendid
shimmied
hill
minute
dinnertime

Other Phonemic-Awareness Activities
for *The Three Little Pigs*

Who's Afraid of the Big Bad Wolf? (sound blending)

The big bad wolf has blown these words apart! Can you sing the tune and put them back together to the melody of *Who's Afraid of the Big Bad Wolf?*

All:
Who in the class can make a word?
> *Make a word?*
> *Make a word?*
Who in the class can make a word?
We can, we can, we can!"

Teacher or volunteer:
/B/ /r/ /i/ /ck/ /s/

Students:
Bricks!

You Built Your House With What? (rhyming)

The three little pigs built their houses with straw, sticks, and bricks. Try to visualize their houses built with other rhyming things.

This little piggy built his house of sticks
> *chicks*
> *wicks*
> *Chex Mix™*

This little piggy built his house of straw
> *coleslaw*
> *jaws*
> *claws*

Other possibilities: rocks, steel, twigs, mud, glass, concrete.
These strange houses are sure fun to illustrate.

Variation: You Built Your House With What? (matching beginning sounds)

Give the students a target sound. Brainstorm a list of materials the pigs may have used to build their houses beginning with the target sound. For example, if /p/ is the target sound:

This little piggy built his house of pineapple
> *popcorn*
> *Pop-Tarts™*
> *posterboard*
> *peanut brittle*
> *plastic*

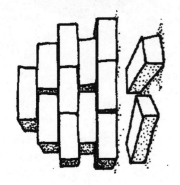

Where the Wild Things Are

Author and Illustrator: Maurice Sendak
(1978) New York: Harper & Row
ISBN: 0-06-443178-9

The Story

Max has an amazing imagination. Your students will love the journey he takes and enjoy making up journeys of their own.

The Sound Board

The pictures represent **Max, king, eyes,** and **claws.**

The Word Lists

Use the following lists and the sound board to teach and reinforce phonemic awareness.

Key:
Italics: words directly from the book
Regular font: other words

Match Rhyming Words

Max	king	eyes	claws
jacks	*thing*	*cries*	paws
wax	ring	*goodbyes*	cause
cracks	wing	spies	grandmas
Big Macs™	ding-a-ling	pies	jaws
tax	spring	rise	laws
facts	fling	wise	gauze
racks	swing	baptize	
Apple Jacks™		flies	

Match Beginning Sounds

Max	king	eyes
Maurice	**claws**	*I'll*
made	*kind*	idle
mischief	*called*	isle
mother	*came*	eye-sore
magic	*cried*	I'd
most	*cross*	icicle
marble	cafeteria	iceberg
melon	cottage cheese	
manufacture	cargo	
makeup	canvas	

Match Ending Sounds

Max	**king**	**eyes**
weeks	*eating*	**claws**
locks	*anything*	*was*
facts	*hung*	*walls*
wax	*waiting*	*things*
specks	gag	*please*
box	bag	*roars*
rocks	chug	*his*
jacks	sling	*vines*
	smorgasbord	

Match Vowel Sounds

Max	**king**	**eyes**	**claws**
/a/	**/i/**	**/i/**	**/aw/**
and	*him*	*wild*	*almost*
that	*anything*	*night*	*all*
an	*in*	*kind*	*called*
gnash	*until*	*cried*	*walls*
magic	*terrible*	*vines*	*fought*
back	*still*	*by*	*caught*
	magic	*private*	*autumn*
	trick	*fly*	*awkward*
	it	*spy*	*chalk*
	things	*try*	*song*
		lied	

Other Phonemic-Awareness Activities
for *Where the Wild Things Are*

Wild Rumpus (sound manipulation)

The wild things "gnash their terrible teeth, roll their terrible eyes, and show their terrible claws." Get your students moving by giving them commands, leaving off a sound for them to fill in before they move.

Roll your terrible ar_!	Students: /M/ *Arms!*
Show your terrible _eet!	Students: /F/ *Feet!*
Twist your terrible _air!	Students: /H/ *Hair!*

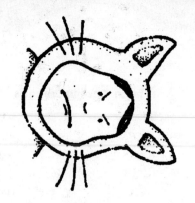

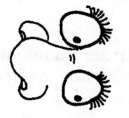

The Paper Bag Princess
Author: Robert Munsch   Illustrator: Michael Martchenko
Toronto, Canada: Annick Press Ltd.

ISBN: 0-920236-82-0

The Story
What a triumph for feminism! Elizabeth, the hero of this book, is a great problem solver and philosopher. Be sure to enjoy many other hilarious books by Robert Munsch with your class.

The Sound Board
The pictures represent **Elizabeth, Ronald,** the **dragon,** and the **cave.**

The Word Lists
Use the following lists and the sound board to teach and reinforce phonemic awareness.

> Key:
> *Italics: words directly from the book*
> Regular font: other words

Match Rhyming Words

Elizabeth	Ronald	dragon	cave
breath	Donald	wagon	gave
death			crave
Seth			brave
Macbeth			grave
			wave
			rave
			save
			misbehave
			microwave

Match Number of Sounds (at the syllable level)

cave	dragon	Elizabeth
(1 syllable)	**Ronald**	**(4 syllables)**
bag	**(2 syllables)**	*magnificent*
clothes	*paper*	incredible
prince	*princess*	embarrassing
breath	*castle*	everlasting
off	*marry*	misbehaving
chase	*carried*	
	something	

back	follow
wear	because
bone	forest
trail	eaten
door	knocker
huge	today
nose	fiercest
world	hundred
wait	nothing
true	seconds
fire	tired
ten	whisper
sleep	ashes
bum	tangled
	pretty

Match Beginning Sounds

Elizabeth	Ronald	dragon	cave
easy	really	dressed	castle
enough	right	drug	clothes
ear	rose	drape	carried
even	rainbow	drawn	could
Easter	risk	drawing	came
eagerly	rapidly	drown	caught
elope	release	drummer	cook
		drop	can

Match Ending Sounds

Elizabeth	Ronald	dragon	cave
with	decided	in	love
breath	find	burn	have
wreath	followed	on	move
beneath	slammed	bone	give
teeth	grabbed	again	brave
Keith	banged	eaten	dove
	hundred	can	glove
	around	ten	shove
	world	even	
	second	when	
	tired	down	
	whispered	open	
	head		
	loud		
	could		

old
tangled
married

Match Vowel Sounds

Elizabeth	Ronald	dragon	cave
/e/	**/o/**	**/a/**	**/a/**
she	*followed*	castle	named
decided	lot	had	chase
because	swallow	smashed	came
he	blah	back	away
eat	hoopla	bag	wait
deep	hurrah	that	lay
even	cottage	have	straight
meat		back	hey
sleep		slammed	paper
ear		grabbed	
neat		can	
		fantastic	
		magnificent	
		ashes	
		after	

Other Phonemic-Awareness Activities
for *The Paper Bag Princess*

Sound Bags (sound matching, rhyming)

❖ Fill a paper bag with several small objects beginning with the same
sound. Have students identify each object as it is pulled out. When the
paper bag is empty, have them label the sound bag. For example, a pencil, paper, peanut, and pit go in a /p/ bag; a ruler, ring, and rope go in a
/r/ bag. Challenge students to decide where they hear the matching
sounds (at the beginning of the words). You might also fill sound bags
with objects that end with the same sound, or objects that rhyme.

❖ Place the sound bags in a center for extended play.

❖ Ask children to bring other objects to put into the sound bags, or to bring
their own sound bag to share.

Guess What's In My Paper Bag (sound blending)

❖ Put one object in each of several paper bags. Tell students the sounds of the word for the object in each bag one at a time. Ask the children to blend those sounds and raise their hands. When hands are up, choose a volunteer to blend the sounds, say the word, and pull the object out of the paper bag. If students are having difficulty blending the sounds, try giving them larger units of sound (onset and rime) and meaning clues. For example, "In this bag, there is a /p/ /en/ /c/ /il/. It is sharp. You use it to write."

❖ Put the paper bags in a center for students to play "Guess What's In My Bag" with each other.

❖ Extend this activity by having students bring their show-and-tell in paper bags for a week. Help each child segment the sounds in their word to play "Guess What's In My Bag" with the class.

Save the Word (sound blending)

❖ Just as Elizabeth tries to save Ronald in *The Paper Bag Princess*, your students try to "save the words." Set a game timer (or count to five). Say sounds for teams to blend into words. (You might target words from the book.) Students lean in and put their heads together to work in whispers. If a team is able to blend the word, everyone on the team raises their hand. Call on the team for the word. If it is correct, the team earns a point and the word is saved. If no team blends the sounds in time, the word is lost.

Variation (sound segmenting)

❖ In this version, students must segment words to "Save the Word." Simply set the timer and say a word. (You might target words from the book.) Students lean in and work together in whispers. They earn a point by breaking the word down into all its sounds. The word is lost if no team makes it in time.

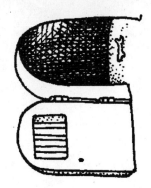

If You Give A Mouse A Cookie

Author: Laura Joffe Numeroff   Illustrator: Felicia Bond
(1985) New York: HarperCollins Publishers
ISBN: 0-694-00416-2
Big Book ISBN: 0-590-64789-X

The Story

A favorite tale for discussing cause and effect. Follow up with Laura Numeroff's take-offs on this book: *If You Give a Moose a Muffin, If You Give a Pig a Pancake,* and the latest, *If You Take a Mouse to the Movies.* Create your own "If you give a _____ a _____". Have you seen the kit *Mouse Cookies:10 easy to Make Cookie Recipes?* (Numeroff and Bond, 1995, HarperCollins) It comes with a mouse-shaped cookie cutter. Celebrate your writing with a cookie shaped like our favorite mouse!

The Sound Board

The pictures represent the **mouse,** the **cookie,** the **straw,** and the **napkin.**

The Word Lists

Use the following lists and the sound board to teach and reinforce phonemic awareness.

Key:
Italics: words directly from the book
Regular font: other words

Match Rhyming Words

mouse	cookie	straw
house	rookie	*draw*
blouse	bookie	seesaw
spouse		caw
clubhouse		jaw
louse		squaw
douse		flaw
outhouse		gnaw
		paw
		outlaw
		Utah
		jigsaw

Match Number of Sounds (at the syllable level)

mouse	**cookie**
straw	**napkin**
(1 syllable)	**(2 syllables)**
give	*going*
milk	*finished*
glass	*mirror*
ask	*mustache*
look	*notice*
hair	*scissors*
trim	*giving*
broom	*carried*
sweep	*every*
room	*washing*
house	*blanket*
floor	*pillow*
nap	*story*
box	*crayons*
crawl	*pictures*
tape	*thirsty*

Match Beginning Sounds

mouse	**cookie**	**straw**	**napkin**
milk	*carried*	*scissors*	*notice*
mirror	*crawl*	*sweep*	*needs*
make	*comfortable*	*start*	*nail*
might	*crayons*	*story*	*nap*
may	kettle	*see*	*name*
means	kitten	*so*	knife
mind	kitchen	*sign*	nestling
mad	climber	*Scotch*	noodle
mingle	cutter	*stand*	nighttime
maneuver	candle	soccer	
machine	ketchup	sandbox	
mannequin		sausage	

Match Ending Sounds

mouse	**cookie**	**straw**	**napkin**
he's	*probably*	*draw*	*when*
glass	*he*	seesaw	*then*
his	*every*	withdraw	*in*
looks	*see*	claw	*even*

needs	*thirsty*	raw	*one*
asks	carry	jaw	*own*
floss	key	hurrah	*crayon*
dress	flee	caught	*sign*
this	spree	sausage	*pen*
fuss	catastrophe		Morgan
blunderbuss			explain
			Gwendelynn

Match Vowel Sounds

mouse	**cookie**	**straw**	**napkin**
/ow/	**/oo/**	**/aw/**	**/a/**
house	*look*	drawl	*ask*
flower	*books*	rawl	*glass*
spout	*looking*	draw	*have*
out	took	want	*mustache*
louder	cook	*drawing*	nap
growl	nook	awful	*blanket*
flounder	shook	all	*stand*
	scrapbook	stall	*back*
		fallen	*hat*
		spawn	*chances*

Other Phonemic-Awareness Activities
for *If You Give a Mouse a Cookie*

If I Give You A Sound (sound manipulation)

Show an illustration from the book. Give students the beginning part of the word pictured (either the syllable, onset, or phoneme). Have students respond with the remainder of the word then blend the parts together.

> *If I give you cook, then you give me _____ /ee/...cookie*
> *If I give you nap, then you give me _____ /kin/...napkin*
> *If I give you /str/, then you give me _____ /aw/...straw*

Other possible words: milk, trim, sweep, nap, pillow, book, picture, refrigerator, thirsty

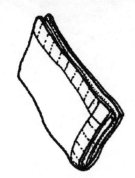

Curious George Rides A Bike
Author: H.A. Rey
(1973) Houghton Mifflin Co.
ISBN: 0-395-17444-9

The Story
Another great tale of the curious little monkey. George gets into trouble but again saves the day and puts on quite a show, too.

The Sound Board
The pictures represent **George,** the **man,** the **hat,** and the **bike.**

The Word Lists
Use the following lists and the sound board to teach and reinforce phonemic awareness.

Key:

Italics: words directly from the book

Regular font: other words

Match Rhyming Words

George	man	hat	bike
forge	*can*	*at*	*like*
gorge	*fan*	*flat*	Mike
	ran	*that*	hike
	began	sat	strike
	plan	brat	
	saucepan	splat	
	catamaran		

Match Beginning Sounds

George	man	hat	bike
gym	my	*he*	be
jig	*men*	*how*	*bag*
jolt	mad	*high*	Bob
jumped	*might*	*hurt*	box
jungle	*moment*	*huge*	bear
juniper	*monkeys*	house	baby
Jupiter	*middle*	*heavy*	boats
	meanwhile	*harder*	bugle
		handed	bronco
		happened	*brightened*

76

Match Ending Sounds

George	man	hat	bike
cage	on	lot	look
rage	fun	out	make
fudge	men	boat	back
bridge	gone	jolt	stuck
	plan	hurt	trick
	blown	first	smoke
	began	float	strike
	again	fleet	magic
	fashion	forgot	pancake
	forgotten	brought	headache
		tonight	
		moment	
		celebrate	

Match Vowel Sounds

George	man	bike
/or/	hat	/i/
for	/a/	why
sorts	cab	tire
corner	bag	time
tractor	last	ride
morning	back	idea
enormous	that	while
	began	cried
	handle	tonight
	standing	sideways
	fashion	bicycle
	animal	delighted
	fanfare	
	breakfast	

Other Phonemic-Awareness Activities for *Curious George Rides A Bike*

Make George Curious (sound matching)

Make George puppets for each child in the group. Enlarge and make copies of George's picture from the sound board. Attach each face to a popsicle stick. Explain that George gets curious and excited (moves up and down, side to side, etc.) when he hears words that match. When words don't match, George isn't curious (puppet stays still). Words might match at the beginning, middle, or end. (You might use words directly from the book.) As you give students a pair (or trio) of words to analyze, make sure they repeat the words aloud.

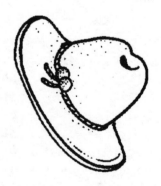

Ten Black Dots
Author: Donald Crews
(1986) NY: William Morrow & Co.
ISBN: 0-688-06067-6
Big Book ISBN: 0-688-13574-9

The Story

Crews' creative counting book gets children to use their artistic imaginations. Put together your own class book by giving students varied numbers of die-cut black dots to make into objects. Then work as a group to write a rhyming text.

The Sound Board

The pictures represent **ten,** the **fox,** the **lace,** and the **train.**

The Word Lists

Use the following lists and the sound board to teach and reinforce phonemic awareness.

Key:

Italics: words directly from the book

Regular font: other words

Match Rhyming Words

ten	fox	lace	train
when	*locks*	*face*	*rain*
seven	rocks	race	brain
again	socks	case	cane
men	flocks	base	main
den	Knox	chase	Jane
then	blocks	space	sprain
bullpen	hawks	bookcase	airplane
pigpen	shocks	disgrace	Elaine
Adrienne	squawks	fireplace	explain
	mailbox		hurricane
	chicken pox		

Match Beginning Sounds

ten	**fox**	**lace**
train	*face*	*locks*
two	*four*	low
turned	*from*	loose
toy	*flowers*	love
tree	*five*	living
tot	*freight*	land
table	*free*	ladybug
tennis	fumble	largest
token	force	leftovers
toothache	finicky	
	fortuneteller	

Match Ending Sounds

ten	**fox**	**lace**
train	*locks*	*dots*
can	six	*eyes*
sun	fix	*keys*
moon	squawks	*snowman's*
when	ox	*beads*
done	rocks	*seeds*
open	box	*flowers*
snowman	peacocks	*knobs*
button	talks	*buttons*
garden	crosswalks	*portholes*
stone		*marbles*
turn		*spots*
nine		*stones*
balloon		*soldiers*
begin		*pennies*
		balloons
		mess
		dress
		confess
		anyplace
		erase

Match Vowel Sounds

ten	fox	lace
/e/	/o/	train
rest	dots	/a/
seven	knobs	make
pennies	spots	day
set	blob	snake
them	lock	rake
pet	clock	freight
rental	hop	eight
said	pond	shake
red	knock	playground
sped	squabble	spacesuit
instead		tray
moped		display
		greyhound

Other Phonemic-Awareness Activities
for *Ten Black Dots*

Cooperative Sound Snakes (sound matching)

❖ Seat students in circles in cooperative teams. Give each team ten black dots (these may be circle shapes or dots cut on a die-cut machine). After dividing the dots among team members, assign a target sound. You might assign one sound for the whole class or one for each team. Each child takes a turn placing a black dot in the middle of the team circle as he or she says a word beginning with the assigned sound. As each word is said, students place the dots side by side to create a sound snake. See how quickly each team can complete their snake with all ten dots. Students can also play by matching ending sounds or rhyming words.

❖ Place the dots in a center for further group play. Individuals may create their own sound snakes. Give students the option of gluing sound snakes to paper and labeling dots with matching words. These make useful classroom alphabet displays. For example: My B snake, Our Ch snake. Sound snakes can also be used to practice letter formation. Students label each dot with the capital or lower case letters representing the target sound.

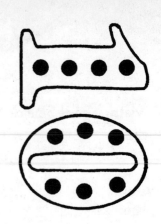

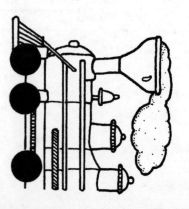

Mary Wore Her Red Dress

Adapter and Illustrator: Merle Peek
(1988) New York: Houghton Mifflin
ISBN: 0-899-19701-9
Big Book ISBN: 0-440-84624-2

The Story

This patterned story about friendly characters going to a birthday party helps youngsters review colors and articles of clothing.

The Sound Board

The pictures represent articles of clothing: a **dress, jeans,** a **shirt,** and a **hat.**

The Word Lists

Use the following lists and the sound board to teach and reinforce phonemic awareness.

Key:

Italics: words directly from the book

Regular font: other words

Match Rhyming Words

dress	jeans	shirt	hat
mess	*green*	dirt	sat
less	bean	Bert	bat
bless	seen	hurt	flat
stress	mean	alert	that
confess	Colleen	flirt	brat
	ravine	insert	

Match Beginning Sounds

dress	jeans	shirt	hat
drape	jar	she	*his*
dragon	jet	shot	*her*
draw	juice	show	hop
drop	jelly	shine	hide
drug	janitor	Shelly	*Henry*
drain	giraffe	shallow	hiccup
drive	jungle		helicopter

Match Ending Sounds

dress	shirt
jeans	hat
his	violet
pants	fit
ribbons	jet
sneakers	what
	felt
	Brett
	blanket

Match Vowel Sounds

dress	jeans	shirt	hat
/e/	/ee/	/ir/	/a/
red	eat	her	as
end	bee	fur	jam
Ben	green	bird	flap
Henry	bleed	stirring	pants
Kenny	feeder	early	grabbed
yellow	Swedish	purple	bandana
sweater		sweater	

Other Phonemic-Awareness Activities
(with reading and writing extensions) for *Mary Wore Her Red Dress*

Clothing Picture Riddles (alliteration)

❖ Focus on the alliterative phrases: "Amanda wore her *brown bandana*. Ryan worn his *purple pants*." Challenge each student to come up with their own combination of a color and piece of clothing beginning with the same sound (green gloves, blue boots). Have your students illustrate their sentences.

❖ Bind the illustrations into a book. Share the picture book with the class or group, asking each illustrator to voice their sound and ask their classmates what piece of clothing it is: For example: /G/ /g/. The group uses this sound clue and the picture to guess the clothing riddle: green gloves.

Clothing Sort (sound matching)

❖ Sort the children according to their clothing and/or garment color. For example, group together children in shorts and shirts; purple and pants; tan and tennis shoes.

❖ Sort clothing picture cards and colors in a pocket chart, then in a center.

Green	Brown	Purple	Shirt
Galoshes	Black	Pants	Shorts
Goggles	Boots		Shoes
Gloves	Barrettes		

If You're Wearing Song (sound matching)

❖ Children will be popping out of their seats with this one. Sing to the tune of "If You're Happy and You Know It:"

If you're wearing something with /sh/ stand right up!
If you're wearing something with /sh/ stand right up!
If you're wearing something with /sh/, then you want to show it off!
If you're wearing something with /sh/ stand right up!
(Children with shirts, shorts, shoes, etc. stand.)

❖ Change the action: If you're wearing something with /p/ shake your head. (Children with the matching article of clothing always stand up to do the action.)

Crazy clothing (phoneme substitution)

❖ As you chant or sing *Mary Wore Her Red Dress*, substitute the beginning sound in each article of clothing with the same beginning sound as its color.

For example,
Mary wore her red ress, red ress, red ress, Mary wore her red ress all day long...
Henry wore his green geakers, green geakers, green geakers...
Katy wore her yellow yeater, yellow yeater, yellow yeater...

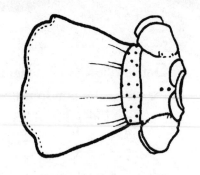

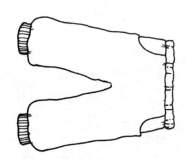

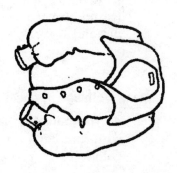

Corduroy
Author: Don Freeman
(1976) New York: Viking Press
ISBN: 0-140-50173-8
Big Book ISBN: 0-14-050173-8

The Story
Children delight in Corduroy's nighttime adventure in search of his lost button. What a comfort when Lisa returns to the store to give this loveable bear a good home. Follow-up by reading *A Pocket For Corduroy* (1978, also in Big Book).

The Sound Board
The pictures represent **Corduroy,** his **overalls,** the **button,** and the **girl** (Lisa).

The Word Lists
Use the following lists and the sound board to teach and reinforce phonemic awareness.

    Key:
    Italics: words directly from the book
    Regular font: other words

Match Rhyming Words

Corduroy	overalls	button	girl
toy	*dolls*	glutton	pearl
boy	calls	mutton	twirl
joy	falls		curl
Troy	malls		hurl
ahoy	enthralls		squirrel
annoy	baseballs		whirl
destroy			unfurl
enjoy			
Illinois			
overjoy			

Match Number of Sounds (at the syllable level)

girl (1 syllable)	button overalls (2 syllables)	Corduroy (3 syllables)
bear	*waited*	*department*
day	*other*	*animals*
green	*morning*	*somebody*
store	*today*	*carefully*
small	*besides*	*amazing*
eyes	*shoulder*	*customer*
strap		*alongside*

lost   sadly   enormous
climb   tonight
bed   mountain
round   palace
bank   mattress
friend   piggy

Matching Beginning Sounds

Corduroy	**overalls**	**button**	**girl**
came	oh!	bear	green
can	over	big	go
climbed	own	buying	gone
could	old	but	gasped
crawled	owner	bright	guess
crash	overjoyed	besides	going
cover	okay	began	get
carried		by	gave
customers		before	garbage
counted		beds	garage
comfortable		both	gamble
		bang	game
		biggest	
		brown	
		bank	
		box	

Match Ending Sounds

Corduroy	**overalls**	**button**	**girl**
toy	dolls	green	fill
boy	animals	then	small
joy	always	one	all
Troy	things	can	animal
ahoy	besides	gone	doll
annoy	eyes	down	little
La Choy™	his	on	I'll
enjoy	shoppers	mountain	table
destroy	doors	brown	crawl
	tables	watchman	pull
	chairs	someone	fell
	sofas	own	topple
	rows	seen	tall
	paws	ran	until
	buttons	began	shall
	freeze	fasten	pal
	energize		

Match Vowel Sounds

Corduroy	overalls	button	girl
/or/	/o/	/u/	/ir/
store	no	was	other
sort	oh!	suddenly	mother
doors	shoulder	under	shoulder
floor	know	escalator	shoppers
morning	go	up	ever
before	so	sofa	overalls
you're	most	palace	searching
four	rows	something	were
enormous	sofa	but	wondered
comfortable	over	until	under
	hello	someone	escalator
	only	watchman	furniture
	own	chum	world
	home	love	heard

Other Phonemic-Awareness Activities
for *Corduroy*

Button Push (sound segmentation, sound blending)

Distribute a handful of buttons to each student. Have the children keep the buttons at the tops of their desks (or in a plastic bag), pulling down only the number you specify. "You need two buttons to begin. Two buttons." (Students place two buttons at the bottom of their desks.) Using words from *Corduroy*, have them push buttons up to the middle of their desks to represent onset and rime, then phonemes. Ask individual students to voice the sounds as they push the buttons. "We are going to say the beginning sound and the chunk in the word *bear*, then use the buttons to push the sounds up to the middle of our desks. Ready?" "/B/" (Push left button upward.) "/ear/" (Push right button upward to join the left button in a row to represent the whole word.) "Run your finger under the buttons and say the word." (Drag finger from left to right.) "*Bear*." (Repeat three times.) "Now let's add one more button. Put the three buttons in a row at the bottom of your desk. Let's say all the sounds in bear, one at a time, as we push our buttons upward. /B/ /ea/ /r/. Now run your finger under the word and say it. Bear." (Repeat three times, segmenting, pushing and voicing the phonemes, then blending them together again.)

When pushing sounds, I like to model with magnets on a magnetic board. I work through several examples with the students, pushing sounds up my board with magnets. Then, I gradually take away that scaffolding, allowing students to try the activity independently. To check each word, a student volunteer comes forward, demonstrating for the group on my magnet board.

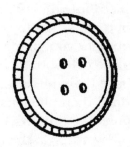

The Very Hungry Caterpillar

Author and Illustrator: Eric Carle
(1984) New York: G. P. Putnam's Sons
ISBN:0-399-20853-4
Big Book ISBN: 0-590-73325-7
(1984) New York: Scholastic

The Story

This story is a favorite for teaching about metamorphosis **and life cycles.**
Share the video version, too.

The Sound Board

The pictures represent the **caterpillar,** the **apple,** the **watermelon,** and the **cheese.**

The Word Lists

Use the following lists and the sound board to teach **and reinforce phonemic** awareness.

    Key:
    Italics: words directly from the book
    Regular font: other words

Match Rhyming Words

caterpillar	apple	watermelon	cheese
miller	Snapple™	felon	bees
filler	grapple	Helen	fleas
thriller		Magellon	skis
killer			trees
			please
			sneeze
			Chinese
			monkeys
			trapeze

Match Number of Sounds (at the syllable level)

cheese (1 syllable)	apple (2 syllables)	caterpillar watermelon (4 syllables)
light	*morning*	supersonic
egg	*Sunday*	thermometer
leaf	*hungry*	thingamajig
pop	*tiny*	somersaulting
sun	*little*	remembering
out	*Monday*	population
ate	*started*	

but	Wednesday	misunderstand	
food	Thursday	relaxation	
look	Friday		
one	pickle		
two	cherry		
pears	sausage		
three	cupcake		
plums	better		
four	cocoon		
five	around		
cake	himself		
cone			
slice			
pie			
night			
big			
fat			
house			

Match Beginning Sounds

caterpillar	apple	watermelon	cheese
came	after	warm	chirp
cake	ant	Wednesday	cheep
cream	antler	wasn't	chicken
cone	antelope	weeks	challenge
cupcake	antenna	walking	champion
cocoon	attitude	wakeful	channel
called	altitude	waterfall	church
		whine	change
		whisper	chores
		wag	chains
			chambermaid

Match Ending Sounds

caterpillar	apple	watermelon	cheese
pear	little	in	was
four	still	moon	plums
after	pickle	one	strawberries
better	small	sun	oranges
speller	nibble	cone	bees
her	hole	again	chimpanzees
glare	beautiful	green	
spare	full	cocoon	
entertainer	smell	than	
score	joyful	eaten	

Match Vowel Sounds

caterpillar	watermelon	cheese
apple	**/aw/**	**/ee/**
/a/	strawberries	very
oranges	small	hungry
that	called	leaf
after	fall	tiny
fat	sprawl	three
than	crawling	he
animals	caught	piece
cantaloupe	automobile	cream
hamburger	gnaw	salami
jam	vault	cherry
bland	sausage	green
cafeteria		weeks

Other Phonemic-Awareness Activities
for *The Very Hungry Caterpillar*

What Sound Did He Eat? (sound segmentation)

The very hungry caterpillar is so hungry; he's eating sounds in words. As you reread the story, students guess what sound is missing from each food the caterpillar eats. For example,

Teacher:	*On Monday, he ate through one /a/__ /l/. What sound did he eat? (Say apple.) What sound is missing?*
Students:	*/p/*
Teacher:	*Where do you hear that sound?*
Students:	*In the middle.*
Teacher:	*On Tuesday, he ate through two __ /ears/. What sound did he eat?"*
Students:	*/p/*
Teacher:	*Where do you hear that sound?*
Students:	*At the beginning.*

Continue reading. If students experience difficulty, have them say the whole word before voicing the missing sound. Also, the task is easier if you work with onsets and rimes instead of phonemes.

For example,
On Wednesday, he ate through three /pl/___/s/.
(The missing chunk is a rime: /um/.)

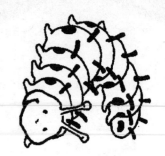

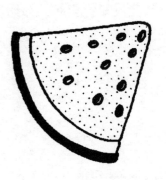

The Napping House
Author: Audrey Wood   Illustrator: Don Wood
(1984) San Diego: Harcourt Brace & Co.
ISBN: 0-152-56708-9
Big Book ISBN: 0-15-256711-9

The Story

What a disruptive sleep pattern! Everyone loves this cumulative tale. Relate this text to other cumulative ones like *Jack's Garden* and *The House that Jack Built*. Have you seen the pop-up version of *The Napping House Wakes Up*?

The Sound Board

The pictures represent the **bed,** the **granny,** the **child,** and the ***flea.***

The Word Lists

Use the following lists and the sound board to teach and reinforce phonemic awareness.

Key:

Italics: words directly from the book

Regular font: other words

Match Rhyming Words

bed	granny	child	flea
red	fanny	mild	*be*
led	nanny	wild	*cozy*
shed		filed	me
instead		smiled	tree
head		styled	free
read		stockpiled	key
shred			spree
ahead			agree
bobsled			Marie
proofread			monkey
gingerbread			teepee
			referee
			guarantee

Match Number of Sounds (at the syllable level)

bed	granny
flea	**child**
(1 syllable)	**(2 syllables)**
and	*wakeful*

on	*snoozing*
that	*dozing*
mouse	*dreaming*
there	*snoring*
can	*cozy*
be	*napping*
cat	*sleeping*
dog	restful
is	behind
who	bedtime
bites	nightlight
scares	
claws	
thumps	
bumps	
breaks	
house	
no	
now	

Match Beginning Sounds

bed	**granny**	**child**	**flea**
bumps	gum	cheer	find
breaks	go	chirp	feed
bites	gift	cheap	fumble
be	get	charcoal	four
barn	guarantee	chimney	forest
blanket	ghost	children	furniture
beast	grumble	chainsaw	fascinate
battlefield	grand	chime	frolic
baseball	gopher		
	Goldilocks		
	Gorilla		

Match Ending Sounds

bed	**granny**
child	**flea**
and	*be*
bend	*cozy*
climbed	*every*
awakened	sleepy
dozed	dreamy
fed	me
flattened	tree
sped	key
fumbled	especially

Match Vowel Sounds

bed	granny	child	flea
/e/	/a/	/i/	/ee/
everyone	and	bites	sleeping
wed	can	white	be
pet	napping	excite	dreaming
letter	slab	night	cozy
web	mad	spine	sweet
medicine	caterpillar	blind	freedom
elevator	vampire	valentine	speedometer
escape	gamble	grapevine	centipede
general	swam	wipe	housekeeping
blender	sandwich	spied	daydream
		inside	moonbeam

Other Phonemic-Awareness Activities
(with reading and writing extensions) for *The Napping House*

Add/Subtract a Sound (phoneme manipulation)

❖ **Adding:** Just as the characters add up in this cumulative tale, students can practice adding phonemes to build words. Distribute unifix cubes. As each sound is added, link cubes to form words.
"Let's start with the word *at*. Make *at* with your cubes." (Students link two cubes together and run a finger under them from left to right while saying *at*.)
"Now lets add a sound to make a new word. Add /p/ at the beginning."
(Students add a cube to represent /p/.)
"Now run your finger under. What's the new word?" (pat)
"What sound did we add?" (/p/)
"Where did we add that sound?" (to the beginning)
"Let's add another sound to build on *pat*. Add /s/ to the beginning."
(Students add a cube to represent /s/)
"Now run your finger. What's the new word? What does spat mean?"

After discussion:
"Now let's add one more sound to make *splat*. What word are we making?" (splat)
"What sound do we need to add?" (/l/)
"Where will that sound be added?" (in the middle)
(Students add a cube to the third position to represent /l/.)
"Now check it with your finger."

Words you might use:

it...pit...pits	ax...wax	all...mall...small	an...ant...plant...plants
in...ink...pink	or...for	is...his...this	us...bus...bust
to...top...stop...stops	ill...hill...chill	in...win...wins	

❖ **Subtracting:** Once the flea wakes the mouse in *The Napping House*, each character is subtracted from the bed in turn. In this manner, students can use unifix cubes to subtract sounds to make new words:

Let's start with four cubes.
(Students link four cubes together to represent the word *twin*.)
Run your finger under the cubes and slowly say the word *twin*.
Now, take off one cube to take away one sound, leaving the word *win*.
What sound must you take away? (/t/)
Where is that sound in the word *twin*? (at the beginning)
Run your finger under the cubes, saying the new word. (*win*)
Now, take off another cube to take away one more sound, leaving the word *in*.
What sound must you take away? (/w/)
Where is that sound in the word *win*? (at the beginning)
Run your finger under the cubes, saying the new word (*in*).

Words you might use:

that...hat...at	*boxes...box...ox*	*pink...ink...in*	*bus...us*
cold...old	*then...hen*	*sled...led...Ed*	*chill...hill...ill*
stop...top	*grant...rant...ant*	*farm...arm*	*spit...pit...it*

Writing Extension:

Adapt the cumulative text by using different characters. Instead of a *dog, flea, child,* and so on, try funny characters. For example, "And on that bed there is a *gorilla*, a snoring *gorilla* on a cozy bed in a napping house, where everyone is sleeping. And on that *gorilla*, there is a *hog*, a drooling *hog*..."

What fun it will be to add these characters on, moving from biggest to smallest, then take the characters off again as they awaken in turn.

Variation (matching beginning sounds)

For more of a challenge add only animals whose beginning sound matches the original character in the book. For example, instead of the granny, it must be a /g/ animal/character, instead of the child, it must be a /ch/ animal/character, etc.

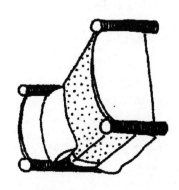

Who's In The Shed

Author: Brenda Parkes   Illustrator: Ester Kasepuu

(1986) Crystal Lake, IL: Rigby

ISBN: 0-76351-102-1

Big Book ISBN: 0-7312-0029-2

The Story

Children delight in this mysterious, repetitive text as they use the clues to guess who's in the shed. I like to stop reading before the conclusion and have students draw and write about who they think is in the shed. Bind their pages, and you have a great class book.

The Sound Board

The pictures represent the **pig,** the **sheep,** the **cow,** and the **horse.**

The Word Lists

Use the following lists and the sound board to teach and reinforce phonemic awareness.

Key:

Italics: words directly from the book

Regular font: other words

Match Rhyming Words

pig	sheep	cow	mare
big	*peep*	*now*	*there*
rig	deep	how	*dare*
swig	weep	sow	*bear*
twig	sweep	bow	*stare*
earwig	cheap	plow	fair
dig	sleep	brow	hair
fig	jeep	chow	flair
sprig	creep	bough	chair
shindig	steep	allow	ensnare
bigwig	asleep	bowwow	beware
	oversleep	eyebrow	compare
	skin-deep	snowplow	nightmare
			everywhere
			millionaire

Match Beginning Sounds

pig	sheep	cow	mare
peep	*shed*	can	*mooed*
pink	*she*	candy	*me*

park	shine	ketchup	mom
pennies	shingle	candlestick	money
people	shepard	canopy	mingle
possum	shotgun	carpenter	machine
possible	shoulder	concentrate	masterpiece
portrait			marathon
postman			

Match Ending Sounds

pig	**sheep**	**cow**	**mare**
howling	pep	*now*	fur
growling	drip	chow	gear
roaring	grump	meow	smear
clawing	cap	anyhow	chandelier
something	escape	somehow	stir
	grape	wow	mother
	stop		carpenter
	cantaloupe		

Match Vowel Sounds

pig	**sheep**	**cow**	**mare**
/i/	**/ee/**	**/ow/**	**/air/**
in	*every*	*now*	*there*
animals	*me*	bow	*dare*
with	*she*	plow	*bear*
did	*see*	allowance	*stare*
little	*sleek*	howdy	flare
pink		crowded	tearing
		howling	parrot
		growling	airport

Other Phonemic-Awareness Activities
for *Who's In The Shed*

Guess Who's In The Shed (sound counting, sound matching, rhyming, sound blending)

Put a plastic animal in a box. Give students clues to the animal's identity. At the end, voice all the sounds for students to blend.

Repeat the following line from the book and give the clues. You might have students call out possibilities after each clue is given or keep their ideas quiet until the end. For example,

Teacher:	*Who's in the shed? everyone said.*
Students:	*Who's in the shed?*
Teacher:	(FIRST CLUE: NUMBER OF SOUNDS) *This animal's name has three sounds.*
	(SECOND CLUE: ENDS WITH) *Its name ends with the /r/ sound.*
	(THIRD CLUE: BEGINS WITH) *Its name begins with the /b/ sound."*
	(FOURTH CLUE: RHYMES WITH) *It rhymes with air.*
	Blend these sounds and you'll have it: /b/ /ea/ /r/.

Open the box and confirm the animal's identity. Have a volunteer choose another animal and help him or her give clues. Place the box and plastic animals in a center for more fun.

Cookie's Week
Author: Cindy Ward   Illustrator: Tomie dePaola
(1988) Putnam Publishing Group
ISBN: 0-399-22406-8
Big Book ISBN: 0-590-56769-1

The Story
Review the days of the week as you follow Cookie's crazy antics. This one is sure to make your students laugh time and time again!

The Sound Board
The pictures represent **Cookie,** the **toilet,** the **drawer,** and some **garbage.**

The Word Lists
Use the following lists and the sound board to teach and reinforce phonemic awareness.

> Key:
> *Italics: words directly from the book*
> Regular font: other words

Match Rhyming Words

Cookie	toilet	drawer	garbage
rookie	pet	more	edge
	wet	*door*	ledge
	met	floor	wedge
	let		
	bet		
	sweat		
	threat		

Match Number of Sounds (at the syllable level)

drawer (1 syllable)	Cookie toilet garbage (2 syllables)
fell	*water*
dirt	*Monday*
plant	*upset*
trash	*kitchen*
stuck	*dishes*
pots	*closet*
pans	*curtains*
rest	

Match Beginning Sounds

Cookie	toilet	drawer	garbage
clothes	*trash*	drove	*got*
climbed	*Tuesday*	drip	game
curtains	*tomorrow*	drug	gate
cut	tot	draw	going
court	tent	drowning	garden
candle	tennis	drapery	gangster
combat	toaster		
counterfeit			

Match Ending Sounds

Cookie	toilet	drawer	garbage
every	*dirt*	more	hedge
maybe	*plant*	*door*	pledge
me	*upset*	*before*	orange
be	*pot*	store	strange
flea	*closet*	ignore	rearrange
free	*went*	dinosaur	stage
stingy	*rest*		age
catastrophe	quietest		village
	parachute		

Match Vowel Sounds

Cookie	toilet	drawer	garbage
/oo/	**/oy/**	**/or/**	**/ar/**
book	toy	*door*	*tomorrow*
shook	foil	*before*	afar
brook	spoil	ore	star
should	oil	tour	Martian
would	broiled	poor	particular
put	pointer	sort	car
	oink	cordless	charcoal
		border	

Other Phonemic-Awareness Activities
(with reading and writing extensions) for *Cookie's Week*

Silly Days of the Week Song (sound manipulation)*

❖ Sing this catchy tune to the beat of *The Adam's Family* theme song. Have the children create funny verses by adding sounds (rimes) to the same beginning sound as each day of the week (see italics).

(refrain)   Days of the week, snap snap
                  Days of the week, snap snap
                  Days of the week, days of the week, days of the week, snap snap.

                  There's Monday, *myday, mayday*
                  There's Tuesday, *tieday, tenday*
                  There's Wednesday, *whyday, winday*
                  Those are silly days!

(refrain)   Days of the week, snap snap
                  Days of the week, snap snap
                  Days of the week, days of the week, days of the week, snap snap.

                  There's Thursday, *thoughtday, thugday*
                  There's Friday, *fishday, funday*
                  There's Saturday, *singday, sandday*
                  And then there's Sunday!

(refrain)

Sing again, creating several silly versions. This makes a great interactive shared reading chart, too. Just write the tune, leaving two blanks after each day of the week. Use sticky notes to fill-in the silly days volunteered or post your own silly days for children to read. A fun related book to read is *Monday, Runday* by Nick Sharratt (Candlewick Press, 1992).

Cookie's Trouble (sound matching)

Cookie gets into different kinds of trouble every day. Challenge students to offer other things Cookie might get into that begin with the same sound of each weekday. For example, on Monday, Cookie may get into mud, mustard, milk, magnets, and so on. These are fun to illustrate and bind into a book, assigning different students different days of the week. Or, you might have children illustrate one page each day of the school week creating a sound book for each day: Cookie's Monday Trouble (all things pictured begin with /m/), Cookie's Tuesday Trouble (all things pictured begin with /t/).

  * Adaptation of the Days of the Week song from the CD: Dr. Jean & Friends, song track #12

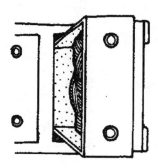

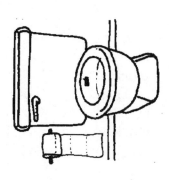

Mrs. Wishy-Washy

Author: Joy Cowley
(1980) Bothell, WA: The Wright Group
ISBN: 1-55911-206-9
Big Book ISBN: 0-7802-7654-X

The Story

Every early childhood teacher knows how kids love *Mrs. Wishy-Washy*. The repetitive, patterned text is easy to learn. My students love to dramatize the story, using great expression for Mrs. Wishy-Washy's lines. It's fun to add extra animals into the story line.

The Sound Board

The pictures represent the **pig,** the **cow, Mrs. Wishy-Washy,** and the **duck.**

The Word Lists

Use the following lists and the sound board to teach and reinforce phonemic awareness.

    Key:

    Italics: words directly from the book

    Regular font: other words

Match Rhyming Words

pig	cow	Mrs. Wishy-Washy	duck
wig	how	she	luck
rig	now	be	muck
dig	plow	free	pluck
big	brow	flea	stuck
fig	sow	tea	chuck
swig	wow		cluck
jig			

Match Number of Sounds (at the syllable level)

pig	(Mrs.)
cow	**wishy**
duck	**washy**
(1 syllable)	**(2 syllables)**
oh	*lovely*
mud	*paddled*
said	*along*
came	*into*
just	*better*

look   *away*
at   muddy
you   listen
tub   upset
go   dirty
went
they

Match Beginning Sounds

pig	cow	Mrs. Wishy-Washy	duck
paddled	*came*	*went*	don't
pot	king	*way*	do
pancake	can	wind	double
possum	capture	wake	deliver
pollute	kind	whisper	door
pen	catch	wonderful	dine
possible	cough	wake	dig
positive	candle	watch	ditches
parent	cop	walrus	dinosaur
panel	couldn't		
pass			

Match Ending Sounds

pig	cow	Mrs. Wishy-Washy	duck
along	how	*lovely*	*look*
gag	sow	*she*	truck
hog	plow	Lee	monarch
log	now	fee	spark
bag	vow	monkey	stuck
eggnog	bow	spree	bark
fog	Moscow	knee	clock
egg		plea	meadowlark
bug		we	paramedic
chug		geography	

Match Vowel Sounds

pig	cow	Mrs. Wishy-Washy	duck
/i/	/ow/	/ee/	/u/
in	how	*screamed*	mud
it	chowder	*she*	lovely
into	rowdy	he	*just*
lid	pouting	free	junkyard
earwig	plow	speed	tunnel

fist	found	cream	spaghetti
visit	meow	beam	hut
pistol	trout	dreamy	lucky
giver	slouch	pleasing	plugging
window	couches	we	

Other Phonemic-Awareness Activities
for *Mrs. Wishy-Washy*

Name Game (alliteration)

Take your cue from Mrs. Wishy-Washy alliterative name. Each student takes a title and an action inspired last name. For example, Devin is Mr. Devin Drawy; Teresa is Ms. Teresa Talky; Sarah is Ms. Sarah Singy, and so on. Students can pantomime their names for others to guess. Create names for people in your school, too.

If You Think You Know This Name (sound blending)

❖ Sing the characters from *Mrs. Wishy-Washy* to the tune of "If You're Happy and You Know It."

If you think you know this name, call it out!
If you think you know this name, call it out!
If you think you know this name, then tell me who it is,
If you think you know this name, call it out!

Teacher: /P/ /i/ /g/
Students: Pig!

❖ **Variation**

Sing characters from other favorite books.
Sing your students names (one of my students' favorite anytime activities!).

110

Five Little Monkeys Jumping on the Bed

Author: Eileen Christelow
(1989) New York: Clarion
ISBN: 0-899-19769-8
Big Book: ISBN: 0-440-84763-X

The Story

This version has a surprise ending! Christelow's illustrations make it delightful. Look for more monkey antics in her other *Five Little Monkeys* books.

The Sound Board

The pictures represent numbers: **five, three, two,** and **zero.**

The Word Lists

Use the following lists and the sound board to teach and reinforce phonemic awareness.

Key:
Italics: words directly from the book
Regular font: other words

Match Rhyming Words

five	three	two	zero
alive	*monkey*	you	hero
jive	we	chew	
drive	see	few	
strive	fee	spew	
thrive	free	clue	
arrive	degree	new	
beehive	happily	true	
high dive	tree	blue	
skydive	spree	renew	

Match Beginning Sounds

five	three	two	zero
fell	*thank*	*took*	zebra
four	thumb	*teeth*	zoo
fast	thimble	toss	Zoro
fur	think	tumble	zany
fun	thought	tonight	zesty
fumbled	thorough	tennis	xylophone
forgotten	thunder	tight	
faked	throwing	table	
fantastic	throat		

Match Ending Sounds

five	three	two	zero
gave	*monkey*	goo	*no*
dove	tree	few	*so*
shove	spree	new	*go*
live	flea	Lou	toe
glove	me	Sue	mow
love	we	true	low
starve	sea	view	Flo
thrive	alimony	blue	bro
survive	money		
groove	funny		

Match Vowel Sounds

five	three	two	zero
/i/	**/ee/**	**/ew/**	**/o/**
bedtime	*she*	you	*no*
night	*teeth*	blew	*so*
I	*sleep*	due	*go*
rice	peace	clue	blow
wise	cheese	grew	grow
find	sheets	ruin	vote
binder	greedy	fluid	boat
trying	speed	chewing	wrote
pliers	seedling	mute	soldier
skyscraper	cheater	neutral	poker
		beautiful	toad

Other Phonemic-Awareness Activities
for *Five Little Monkeys Jumping on the Bed*

Sing in Rounds (rhyming)

Sing the song of *Five Little Monkeys*. To focus your children on rhyme, follow these directions for each round.

> ***Round One:*** Instead of singing the rhyming words, clap for each.
> *Five little monkeys jumping on the (clap). One fell off and broke his (clap)...*
> ***Round Two:*** Instead of singing the rhyming words, pantomime.
> *Five little monkeys jumping on the* (hands sweep imaginary covers). *One fell off and broke his* (point to head). *Mamma called the doctor and the doctor* (mouth moves like talking). *No more monkeys jumping on the* (hands sweep covers).
> ***Round Three:*** Clap the beat. Only sing the rhyming words.
> ***Round Four:*** Sing new rhyming words. (You might do several different versions.)
> *Five little monkeys jumping on the couch. One fell off and he said, "Ouch." Mama called the doctor and the doctor said, "No more monkeys jumping on the couch."*

Monkey Business (sound matching, rhyming)

Use the game "Barrel of Monkeys." Students must give matching words to connect the monkeys. For example, make a monkey chain of /s/ words, /ing/ words, words that end in /k/, and so on.

Hint: If you don't have the game, you might play using other objects that link like metal rings or paper cups.

Variation (sound manipulation)

Have students change one sound to make a new word in order to connect their monkeys. For example, if the first monkey is *fun*, the connecting monkey could be *sun*, then *run*, then *ran*, then *man*, then *men*, then *hen* and so on.

114

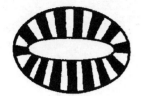

Bread and Jam for Frances

Author: Russell Hoban   Illustrator: Lillian Hoban

(1993) New York: HarperCollins Juvenile Books

ISBN: 0-060-22359-6

Big Book ISBN: 0-06-443336-6

The Story

Frances' little rhymes will amuse your students and give them lots of practice identifying rhyming words. Every child can learn from Frances' tale. Remember: "Variety is the spice of life!"

The Sound Board

The pictures represent **Frances,** the **bread,** the **jam,** and the **egg.**

The Word Lists

Use the following lists and the sound board to teach and reinforce phonemic awareness.

Key:

Italics: words directly from the book

Regular font: other words

Match Rhyming Words

Frances	bread	jam	egg
dances	*said*	*am*	peg
prances	*salad*	ham	leg
lances	*spread*	ram	nutmeg
	lead	gram	beg
	med	lamb	Greg
	ahead	Shazzam	
		Uncle Sam	

Match Number of Sounds (at the syllable level)

bread	Frances
jam	**(2 syllables)**
egg	*breakfast*
(1 syllable)	*eating*
soft	*without*
sang	*inside*
slide	*spreading*
spoon	*funny*
slice	*sunny*
plate	*stomach*

fork
school
lunch
rope
toast
treat
beans
veal
dish
taste
juice
cheese

scrambled
skipping
biscuits
berry
dinner
cutlet
nightgowns
chicken
sandwich
meatballs
Albert

Match Beginning Sounds

Frances	**bread**	**jam**	**egg**
father	breakfast	just	everyone
fond	baby	juice	anything
funny	boiled	joy	end
fall	but	jar	everywhere
fork	books	junk	episode
from	box	jelly	envelop
French	bus	juniper	energetic
flannel	biscuits	Julie	enemy
furry	beans	jacks	
friend	baked	jester	
filled	bite	jungle	
folded	bottle		
fast	bunch		
full	began		
favorite	bell		
	black		
	basket		

Match Ending Sounds

Frances	**bread**	**jam**	**egg**
lots	boiled	time	eating
course	slide	handsome	thing
stomachs	inside	from	song
bus	could	cream	sang
biscuits	did	home	spreading
cutlets	side	some	string
jackets	scrambled	am	anything
suits	trade	plum	nothing
else	salad	come	morning

117

thermos	*custard*	*them*	*rang*
guess	*around*		*running*
glass	*sprinkled*		*pudding*
sauce	*spread*		*helping*
goodness	*playground*		

Match Vowel Sounds

Frances	**bread**
jam	**egg**
/a/	**/e/**
glass	breakfast
jackets	yes
scrambled	salad
fast	spread
flannel	them
sandwich	anything
asked	stomachs
have	goodness
that	said
raspberry	end
handsome	well
had	
can	
at	

Other Phonemic-Awareness Activities
(with reading and writing extensions) for *Bread and Jam for Frances*

Silly Sandwiches (alliteration)

❖ Shel Silverstein's (1974) poem "Recipe For A Hippopotamus Sandwich" makes a great kick-off for this activity. It begins, "A hippo sandwich is easy to make. All you do is simply take..." (pg. 115). Since Frances only liked jam on her sandwich, challenge students to create silly sandwiches made of things Frances would definitely pass up. Assign each child, pair of children, or group a sound. Instruct them to describe their sandwich focusing on that sound. For example, "A cheery sandwich is easy to make. All you do is simply take...ten Cheerios™, Chee tos™, lots of Chap Stick™. Chill before eating." Or... "A pumpkin sandwich is easy to make. All you do is simply take...a ripe pumpkin, peanuts, piles of peels, paper and pencils. Put them in a pita."

❖ Kids love illustrating their silly sandwiches.

Variations (rhyming)

❖ Create silly sandwiches by using only rhyming words! "A jam sandwich is easy to make. All you do is simply take…jam, ham, a little spam. Cram them in a frying pan. Serve them to your buddy Sam."

❖ Frances' Food Funnies: Throughout the story, Frances makes up funny rhymes about food. After rereading each of her verses, clap and repeat the rhyming words. After playing with these rhymes, encourage students to create their own. Write them down. Sing them. Make a "Food Funnies" rhyming class book.

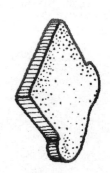

More Activities and Extensions

The following activities will help your students internalize the principles of phonemic awareness and will help you extend sound-board lessons throughout the curriculum.

Listening for Sounds

After focusing on meaning for years, it's a foreign notion to our young students to start listening *inside* words for sounds. What does it mean to listen for sounds? Since phonemic awareness is an abstract concept, it's useful to provide children with concrete, visual models. The following activities help increase students' understanding of what phonemic awareness is, why it is important, and how and when to use their skills.

❖ **Unifix cubes: break them apart, put them together:** One method for making the idea of listening for sounds concrete is to use a row of connected unifix cubes to represent a whole word. As you demonstrate how to break words down, break away cubes from the row to represent sounds. Put the cubes back in place as you blend the sounds back together to make a whole word.

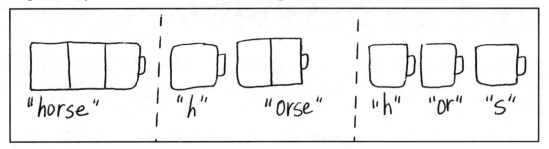

Hold up the row of unifix cubes: "This represents a whole word. Let's pretend this is the word *horse*. (Run your finger under the whole word, moving from students' left to right view while slowly voicing /hhhooorrrssse/.) If I listen carefully, saying the word slowly, I can hear the beginning sound in horse. /Hhhhhh/ (run finger under the first cube, breaking it away from the row) /orse/ (run finger under the remainder of the row)." Demonstrate how to blend the beginning sound and the rime back together while reassembling the cubes. Further, segment the phonemes in the word, while breaking the row apart (/h/ /or/ /s/). Blend the phonemes back together again and reassemble the cubes. This creates a visual model using something concrete to show what we mean and what we are actually doing when we segment words into sounds and blend sounds to make words.

Another way to visually represent the same thing is to use a piece of construction paper as the whole word, taking scissors to cut the whole apart as you listen for and segment sounds. Or try spiral rings. They link together and come apart easily.

During interactive writing, use the row of cubes (or spiral rings or construction paper) to break down words, hear sounds, and represent them with letters on paper: "We hear /h/ first. What letter do we need? Who can make the letter *h*?" Voila! Children finally *see* what you mean when you ask, "What's the beginning sound? What does it start with? What do you hear? Break the word apart. What's the middle sound? What's the ending sound?"

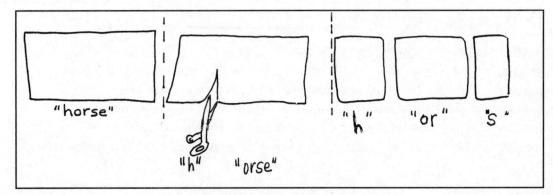

❖ **Sound Puppets:** On a trip to a conference, I bought little cat puppets at one of the vender displays. Three different colored kittens sit in one basket. I put in three fingers, and they become a lively bunch of kittens. When trying to break down words during interactive writing, I often grab the "Sound Cats." We say the word slowly. The first cat wiggles and bends forward for the first sound, the second cat bends for the middle sound, and the third cat bends for the ending sound. As we segment the sounds with the cats, we share the pen to represent each sound with a letter. Then, I bend them quickly in turn to blend the sounds back together to say the whole word (Figure 12). My kids adore these puppets, often asking, "Pleeeeease, can we use the sound cats?"

My sound cats.

If you don't have the good fortune of owning such puppets, you can use other finger puppets. You can purchase them at party-supply stores or make them out of paper. Kids appreciate having their own set of paper puppets to use during sound play, and they are a great aid for any kind of writing. Many exquisite finger puppets are available from Folkmanis, Inc. (www.folkmanis.com).

❖ **Kid Smush:** Kid smush is another way to represent blending and segmenting words. The only materials required are your students. Call forward enough students to represent each sound in a word. For example, four students could represent *smile*, three students could represent *cow.* Smush the students together in a row shoulder to shoulder. "This is the whole word *cow.*" As you work with the students to segment the word into sounds, pull each student away from the row. I like to be very dramatic, tugging, saying the sound slowly, while breaking the students out of the row. "I hear /ccccccccc/. This must be the beginning sound in /ccccc-cow/." Continue segmenting, breaking away each sound and student in turn. Smush the students back together again to reblend the sounds and re-create the whole word.

Kid smush is another great way to break down words and represent sounds with letters during writing.

❖ **Push the Sounds:** Elkonin boxes (Elkonin, 1973) are another handy tool to use during interactive writing. Draw one box for each sound in the word you are writing. Push your finger into each box as you voice the word slowly. Then, do it again, having students add letters for each sound they hear. If they get stuck, fill in the letter(s) yourself. Transfer the spelling from the sound boxes to the interactive writing chart.

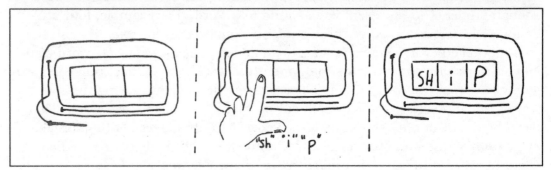

Magna Doodle with Elkonin boxes.

I like to draw the boxes on a Magna Doodle™, white board, or small chalkboard. They are portable and easy to clean so we are always ready to work through tough words.

Elkonin boxes support individual students as they work to spell words during Writing Workshop, too. You can also teach students to draw their own sound boxes when they are stuck on words. Some teachers tape record directions for the technique so that, during center time, students can push buttons into boxes for the sounds they hear in words.

Fitting Sound Boards to Other Literature

Several of the sound boards might be adapted for use with other books or literary selections such as poems or chants. This is best with boards that have generalizable themes such as:

- ❖ **numbers:** *Five Little Monkeys Jumping On The Bed*
- ❖ **foods:** *The Very Hungry Caterpillar, If You Give A Mouse A Cookie*
- ❖ **animals:** *Brown Bear, Brown Bear, What Do You See?, Who's In The Shed?, I Know An Old Lady Who Swallowed A Fly*
- ❖ **clothing:** *Mary Wore Her Red Dress*

For example, after learning a counting chant in math or reading the book *A Big Fat Hen* (Baker, 1994), use the Five Little Monkeys board for sound play. This board features numbers as column headers.

You can fold back columns to make a board more adaptable. Fold back the teacher from the Brown Bear board or the caterpillar from the Very Hungry Caterpillar board and you have two widely useable boards. Or, fold under the bike column on the Curious George board, and you have a board you can use with any of the Curious George books. When teaching students the chant "Who Stole the Cookie from the Cookie Jar?" (one of my personal favorites), fold under the mouse column from *If You Give A Mouse A Cookie*, and work with the words cookie, milk, and napkin. Fold the columns back before copying, or, if they have already been copied, just fold them under.

Using Sound Boards for Phonics

After using the sound boards to match beginning and ending sounds, extend the lesson into letter–sound correspondence and letter formation practice. Begin by quickly reviewing answers in each column:

That's right pot, party, pocket *and* paste *all start with the same sound as* pig. *So, you have four markers in that column.*

Which letter makes that sound? (Repeat the sound as necessary.)

Demonstrate the letter formation on the chalkboard or overhead. Then ask students to practice writing the letter and to trace and retrace it, using different colored crayons (rainbow writing). Each time students write or trace the letter, encourage them to repeat some words from the matching column, offer other like-sounding words, and repeat the sound in isolation (/p/ /p/ /p/). (For further ideas see "Connecting to Classroom Word Walls.")

Connecting Sound-Board
Knowledge to Reading and Writing

It's not enough for children to learn sounds, letter names, and letter formations. They must learn how to apply this knowledge to read and write words. Snow, Burns, and Griffin (1998) list this as a goal for every grade level, including kindergarten: Students must "use phonemic awareness and letter knowledge to spell independently (invented or creative spelling)." One way of emphasizing this connection is to extend sound-board lessons into writing and reading. Some examples,

Focus on beginning cues for writing:

Teacher: *Ok, we know pig begins with the /p/ sound, like pot and pineapple (write pig on the chalkboard or overhead, underlining p), and cow starts with /k/, like ketchup and card (write cow on the chalkboard or overhead, underlining c). If I'm writing about my cats, which word would help me? Try them: cats—cow, cats—pig. Which word has the matching beginning sound? Which word will help me write cats?*

Students: *Cow!*

Teacher: *Yes, cow begins like cats. They both start with the /k/ sound. When words sound the same at the beginning, they often are spelled with the same letter. If this is pig and this is cow (pointing to the written words on the chalkboard) which letter would I need to begin to write the word cats?*

Students: *c!*

Teacher: *Yes! Now write c on your paper.*

Make this lesson more advanced by giving students three or four words to compare to the word they're trying to write. For example: "If I am writing an informational book about dinosaurs, which word would help me (pointing to the written choices on the board: *pig, cow, duck,* or *Mrs. Wishy-Washy*)?"

Sum up by stating the purpose of the lesson: "That's why we practice with our sound boards. If you can hear how words sound the same, you can use the spelling of one word to help you write another."

...and reading:

Teacher: *We know that pig begins with /pppp/ p and cow begins with /kkkk/ c (pointing to these words and underlined letters on the chalkboard). If I were reading a book and came across this word (write on chalkboard or overhead, but do not say the word) penguin, how would I begin to sound it out? What word does it look like, pig or cow?*

Students: *pig!*

Teacher: *Yes, pig begins with the same letter as this word (pointing to penguin). And what sound does that letter make?*

Students: /p/!

Teacher: *Right! So, this word must begin with /ppp/. Then, I could check the picture to see if that helps (begin to draw a picture clue to help children identify the word). What do you think the word is?*

Students: Penguin.

Explore a few more examples; but not too many. Short, frequent mini-lessons like this are very powerful over time. When students are highly successful choosing from two words, increase to three and then four possible words. Remember, this type of activity works well with small groups.

Sum up by stating the purpose of the lesson: "That's why we practice with our sound boards. If you can hear how words sound the same, you can use a word you know to help you read another."

Focus on ending cues for writing:

As students start to use beginning sounds and letters to read and write new words, it's appropriate to turn their attention to ending sounds and letters. You can vary the mini-lessons above for this purpose. Here are some samples:

Teacher: *We marked our columns as we matched ending sounds. We know pig ends with /ggggg/ like dug and leg (write pig on the chalkboard, underlining g) and duck ends with /kkkk/ like bark and sick (write duck on the chalkboard underlining k). Which word—piggg or duckkk would help me write the ending sound in the word like? How do you know? What will that look like? Now, try on your paper.*

...and for reading:

Teacher: *We know pig ends in /ggggg/ (point to pig and the underlined letter g) and duck ends with /kkkk/ (point to duck and k). If I came across this word in a book (write, but do not say the word bug) and I already knew the beginning sound, what else might help me figure out the word? What word do we know that ends with the same sound? Does the letter at the end look the same? The picture may also help me (begin to draw a picture clue to help students identify the word).*

Adapt the difficulty of the lessons by giving students more words to choose from. Again, fast and frequent is my motto. Rather than doing too many examples in one lesson, many brief demonstrations make a real difference over time.

Focus on chunks (rimes):

Students who are using beginning and ending letters to read and write words will benefit from learning how to use chunks. After marking sound-board columns for rhyming words and identifying ending chunks (rimes, phonograms, word families) in the column-header words, lead students to connect their knowledge of sounds to reading and writing.

... for writing:

Teacher: *We know brick has the ick chunk (write brick on the chalkboard or overhead, underlining ick) like stick and lick, and straw has the aw chunk (write straw on the chalkboard or overhead, underlining aw), like ma and coleslaw. If I am writing about a trick I did in gymnastics, which word would help me? Brick or straw?*

Students: Brick!

Teacher: *Yes! Brick and trick rhyme. They have the same ending chunk —ick. When words rhyme, the chunk at the end is often spelled the same. Who can come to the chalkboard and give trick a go? (Support the volunteer in writing trick under the word brick. Then ask the class:) How did we do?*

Yes, if this is brick with the ick chunk, /i-c-k/, then trick must be spelled t-r-i-c-k. Now you try writing trick on your paper.

Complete other examples. When students are highly successful at choosing from two words, give them a choice of three or four. This is an activity that works well with small groups.

Sum up: "We practice listening for rhyming words with our sound boards because if you can hear how words rhyme, you can use the spelling of one word to help you write another."

...and for reading:

Teacher: *Brick has the ick chunk (point to brick and ick) and straw has the aw chunk (point to straw and aw). Which would help me read this word if I came across it in a book? (Write draw on the board.) Which word has the same ending chunk? What is that sound? So, what is this word?"*

Be sure to include multisyllabic examples, as well:

Teacher: *Which word would help me read this word? (Write sticker on the chalkboard.) How do you know? What's the sound? Are there any other chunks you know in this word?...*

Give students more words to choose from to increase difficulty. Keep the lessons fast and focused.

Sum up: "We practice listening for rhyming words with our sound boards because if you can hear how words rhyme, you can use words you know to read new words."

Connecting Sound Board to Classroom Word Walls

You can easily connect sound boards to classroom word walls.

When you're matching beginning and ending sounds on the sound boards, draw attention to key words with the same sounds on your ABC Wall and/or Name Wall (see Wagstaff, 1997; 1999). For example, "Yes, *purple* matches with *pig* because it begins with /pppp/, just like *Payton* on our Name Wall." "Yes, *rock* ends like *duck*. Good job matching the ending sound! What word do we know that has the /kkkk/ sound from our word wall?"

When matching rhyming words, refer to your Chunking Wall (Wagstaff, 1994; 1995;

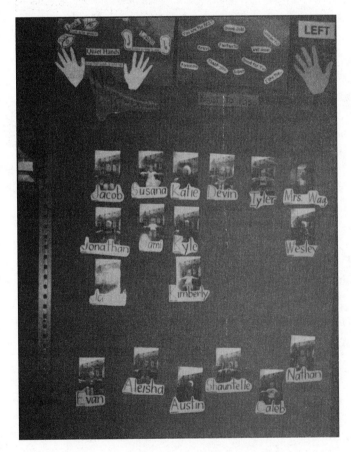

1999). "You matched *brick* with *slick*. Both have the *ick* chunk like *trick* on our Chunking Wall." These quick references are especially helpful during the reading and writing analogy mini-lessons just described (pages 126-128). The more you refer to your word walls, the more natural it will be for your students to use them.

If you are not already building word walls, the books that match the sound boards here make great contexts for examining how words work. You can enlarge column-header pictures on the copy machine and use them as key-word clues for the Name, ABC, or Chunking Walls (Wagstaff, 1999). For example, *Curious George, Mrs. Wishy-Washy, Viola Swamp,* and *Yoko* could represent /g/, /w/, /v/, and /y/ respectively on a Name Wall alongside your students' names.

❖ **Name Wall and Name Sound Board:** Like many teachers, I begin the school year focusing on students' names, playing "get-to-know-you" games. Photos of students with their names written underneath and the beginning letter highlighted in red serve as our Name Wall. We use the beginning and ending sounds in names to make analogies for reading and spelling (see Wagstaff, 1999). One morning at the beginning of the school year, I awoke to the realization I could heighten students' phonemic awareness by adapting my sound-board idea to incorporate students' names. I chose four children, copied and trimmed their photos. Four faces become the column headers.

We match words to names based on rhyme, beginning sounds, and ending sounds, just as we work with any other sound board. What an easy and effective way to capitalize on students' interest in names (and photos of themselves and classmates), make ties to the beginning-of-the-year curriculum, and develop phonemic awareness.

Sound Matching with Class Photos: Say a word that begins with one of the pictured students' names. Ask students to repeat the word and the names pictured, listening for the name that begins with the same letter. Students place a marker (unifix cube, penny, or other object) in the column of the match. You can also try this by matching ending sounds.

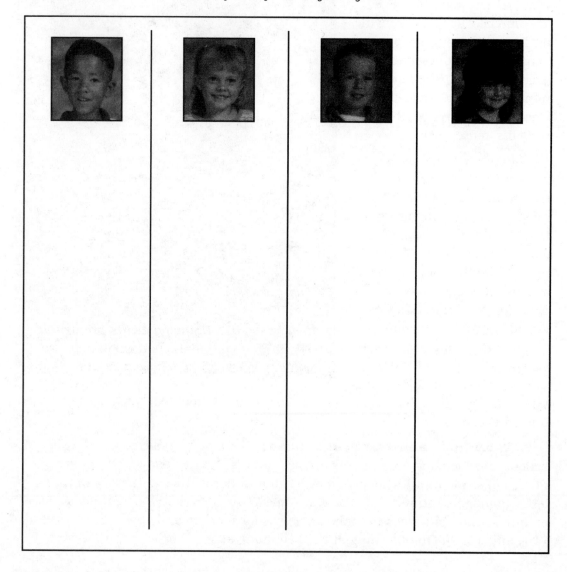

Maximizing Class Time

We are all pressed for time with so much to teach. Make the most of your classroom minutes by incorporating the ideas below.

Sound-Board Audiotapes—Centers and Take-homes

When you're working with the whole class, a small group, or an individual on a sound-board lesson with a clear phonemic-awareness focus, consider tape recording the session. You can place the tape and accompanying materials in a sound center for students to use on their own. Students can also take the package home. (You can send home the family letter, from Appendix B, and introduce this idea at "Back to School Night" and parent conferences). Recording sessions for use in centers or as take-home activities, provide extra practice without requiring much additional time or preparation.

Include in the package (a gallon-size plastic bag):

❖ the audiotape

❖ copies of the sound board

❖ manipulatives such as unifix cubes, coins, beans, or edibles

❖ copies of the book, rhyme, or chant (optional).

The plastic bags may be stored to use again and again.

Sample audiotape lesson:

We enjoyed the book, Mrs. Wishy-Washy, *together. Remember some of the characters in the book? Look at the top of your sound board. Point as I say the name of each character: pig, cow, Mrs. Wishy-Washy, and duck. Say their names with me as we point again: pig, cow, Mrs. Wishy-Washy, duck. Great!*

Today we'll be listening for rhyming words. Rhyming words are words that sound the same at the end like hit *and* spit; make *and* cake; hen *and* pen. *Let's try to match some rhyming words with the characters at the top of your sound board. Ready?*

Let's try one together. The word to match is luck. *Say* luck—l-uck. *Which word rhymes with* luck? *Let's test each column. Say the words with me.* Pig—luck; cow—luck; Mrs. Wishy-Washy—luck; duck—luck. *Which word rhymes or sounds the same as* luck *at the end? Put a marker in the column of the word that rhymes with* luck. *Yes, say* duck *and* luck, duck—luck. *Hear how these words rhyme.*

Let's try another word. The word to match is big. *Say* big—b-ig. *Which word rhymes with* big? *Let's test them together. Say* pig—big; cow—big; Mrs. Wishy-Washy—big; duck—big. *Which word rhymes with* big? *Put a marker in the column of the word that rhymes with* big. *Did you hear it?* Pig *and* big *rhyme. Say* pig *and* big. *Good! You should have one marker under* duck *and one marker under* pig. *Let's keep testing rhyming words...."*

Transition Time

Use times between activities to throw in a little phonemic-awareness practice. For example, when asking students to line up or come to group, you might give them directions that involve sound matching, blending, or segmenting. Or, try sound matching, blending, phoneme substitution, or rhyming when passing out materials. Here are some examples of quick phonemic awareness activities you can use to move students around the room:

SOUND MATCHING:

Beginning sounds:	*Line up if your name begins with the same sound as* baseball.
Ending sounds:	*Line up if your name ends like...*
Rhyming words:	*Line up if your name rhymes with...*

SOUND BLENDING:

Syllables:	*Table one, put these two word parts together to come to the rug:* /re/ /cess/.
Onset and rime:	(Same as above, except harder.../r/ /e/ /c/ /ess/)
Phonemes:	(Same as above, still harder.../r/ /e/ /c/ /e/ /s/)

SOUND SEGMENTING:

Phonemes:	*First choice for centers goes to the team who can break the word* read *into its smallest sounds, beginning sound, middle sound, and ending sound:* read.
Onset and rime:	(Same as above, except easier.../r/ /ead/)
Syllables:	(Same as above, except easier.../ead/ /er/)

Here are phonemic awareness activities you can use when you're passing out materials:

SOUND MATCHING:

Ending sounds:	*Look at these masks of the characters from* Mrs. Wishy-Washy. *If you want to be the character whose name ends with /k/ raise your hand. Which character is it?*
Beginning sounds:	*Which character's name begins with /d/?*

SOUND BLENDING:

Phonemes:	*This folder belongs to /D/ /e/ /v/ /i/ /n/."* (Kids) "Devin!"
Chunks or syllables:	(Same as above except easier.../Dev/ /in/)

PHONEME SUBSTITUTION:

Beginning sounds:	*I'll say your names with /j/ today. When you hear your name, come up for your materials. Jark.* (Kids) "Mark!"
Ending sounds:	(Same as above, except substitute ending sound... /ch/...Mark = March)
Rhyming:	*I have someone's paper here. Her name rhymes with the word* play. (Kids) "Shay!"

Phonemic-Awareness Songs:

Another time-saving and fun way to practice matching, blending, and segmenting sounds is through music. Yopp (1992) wrote about the idea of taking familiar tunes and changing them for sound play. For example, take a tune like "If You're Happy and You Know It" and sing, "If you think you know this friend, yell it out!" After singing the verse, voice a student's name in phonemes like /J/ /a/ /ce/. The students blend and yell out the name: "Jace!" You can record these sound-singing sessions and use them in a listening center or send them home for more practice.

You can find other song ideas in the Yopp article cited above and the following books:

Phonemic Awareness: Playing with Sounds to Strengthen Beginning Reading Skills (1997) by Fitzpatrick, J. From Creative Teaching Press.

Phonemic Awareness Songs and Rhymes (three book series) (1998) by Jordano, K. and Callously-Jones, T. From Creative Teaching Press.

Phonemic Awareness: Songs and Rhymes (1999) by Wiley Blevin. From Scholastic, Inc. 800-724-6527

ABC Chick Boom with Me (1999) by John Archambault and David Plummer. From Creative Teaching Press.

INVOLVING OTHERS

Besides getting parents involved (see the parent letter in Appendix B), you can maximize your class time by involving volunteers (use the volunteer-instruction letters from Appendix B) in small-group or individual sound play. You can do this by creating sound packages or extending the use of your sound boards by organizing them for volunteers.

Create sound packages:

Write simple instructions for a phonemic-awareness activity on an index card. Gather any necessary hands-on materials like unifix cubes, geometric shapes, popsicle sticks, and so on. Place the instructions and materials in a plastic bag. When volunteers arrive, give them the all-inclusive sound package and a group of

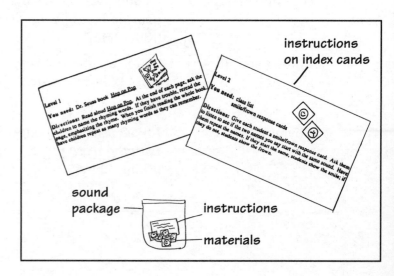

students and off they go! Make sure the volunteers know they'll be working with students on *oral* activities, helping them refine their skills in hearing and manipulating sounds in spoken words.

A handy resource for creating sound packages is Jo Fitzpatrick's book, *Phonemic Awareness: Playing with Sounds to Strengthen Beginning Reading Skills* (1997; Cypress, CA: Creative Teaching Press). The book has leveled task cards for sound games. Copy the cards, gather the materials, and place each activity in a plastic bag.

Filing Systems:

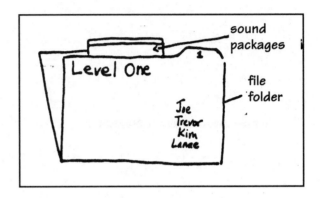

File the bag as according to skill level (level ones in one file folder, and so on) and print students' names in pencil on the front of the file to indicate flexible groupings (Phonemic-awareness skill levels are detailed on Pg 1, Appendix B). Again, when volunteers arrive, everything is ready to go. You might have the volunteer do one activity with each group.

You can extend the use of your sound boards by filing them in sets and attaching simple instructions (Appendix B) for volunteers on the front of each file. Include a bag of unifix cubes or edibles inside your file drawer. When a volunteer arrives, grab the file and bag of edibles, give them a group, and they're ready to work.

Sound Charts

There are two main purposes for the Sound Charts that follow:

❖ **To provide a handy reference so teachers can match target sounds to book titles and sound boards.** For example, if teaching about /m/, teachers can quickly see which sound board(s) apply.

❖ **As a reminder that *we are working with sounds* regardless of spelling.** In the second column ("as in..."), notice the many ways sounds can be spelled, and be aware that the column only contains some of the ways that a sound may be spelled. What does this mean for teaching? It means that when we say words for children to match, it's essential to stretch our thinking beyond traditional, simple spellings. For example, if the objective is to match the long <u>u</u> sound, think beyond words spelled simply with u or the u-e pattern. Long <u>u</u> may be spelled with *u* like in *ruby*, *u-e* like in *rude*, *ui* like in *fruit*, *ew* like in *grew*, *o* like in *move*, *oo* like in *pool*, *ou* like in *troupe*, *ough* like in through, and so on. When I think up words for students to match, I play with the sound in my head—keeping thoughts of spellings at bay.

When you stretch the use of sound boards into phonics/spelling/writing (for example, sending a board home for children to write matching words in columns), you can explain that sounds can have varied spellings. Such opportunities help children learn to be flexible when dealing with the spellings of sounds.

Phoneme Consonants	as in...	Sound Boards to match beginning sounds	Sound Boards to match ending sounds
/b/	bat, brat, bubble	I Know An Old Lady, Brown Bear, Wheels On The Bus, The Napping House, Curious George, Corduroy, Three Little Pigs, Bread and Jam for Frances	
/k/ /c/	cat, quiet, duck, chorus	Mrs. Wishy-Washy, Who's In The Shed? Cookie's Week, Animals Should Definitely Not, Paper Bag Princess, If You Give A Mouse, Very Hungry Caterpillar, Where The Wild Things Are, Corduroy	Lilly's Purple Plastic Purse, Mrs. Wishy-Washy, Jack's Garden, Miss Nelson Is Missing, Wheels On The Bus, Curious George, Three Little Pigs, Yoko, The Snowy Day
/d/	dog, held, ladder	Mrs. Wishy-Washy, I Know An Old Lady, Wheels On The Bus, Ten Black Dots	Jack's Garden, I Know An Old Lady, Paper Bag Princess, Wheels On The Bus, The Napping House, Bread and Jam for Frances
/f/	fish, fluff, phone, laugh	Five Little Monkeys, The Napping House, Yoko, Ten Black Dots, Bread and Jam for Frances, Brown Bear	Animals Should Definitely Not, Three Little Pigs
/g/	gal, egg, ghost	I Know An Old Lady, Cookie's Week, The Napping House, Curious George, Corduroy	Mrs. Wishy-Washy, Who's In The Shed?, I Know An Old Lady, Curious George, Three Little Pigs, Bread and Jam for Frances
/h/	he, whose	Who's In The Shed?, I Know An Old Lady, Animals Should Definitely Not, Miss Nelson Is Missing, Curious George, Mary Wore Her Red Dress	
/j/	jam, giraffe, judge, soldier	Jack's Garden, Animal's Should Definitely Not, Bread and Jam for Frances, Mary Wore Her Red Dress	Cookie's Week
/l/	lip, bell, apple	Lilly's Purple Plastic Purse, Ten Black Dots	Very Hungry Caterpillar, The Snowy Day
/m/	man, climb, common	Brown Bear, If You Give A Mouse, Where The Wild Things Are, Curious George	Bread and Jam for Frances
/n/	nap, knit, gnash	Miss Nelson is Missing, If You Give A Mouse	Jack's Garden, Animals Should Definitely Not, Paper Bag Princess, Miss Nelson Is Missing, Very Hungry Caterpillar, If You Give A Mouse, Wheels On The Bus, Curious George, Corduroy, Ten Black Dots

Phoneme Consonants	as in...	Sound Boards to match beginning or medial sounds	Sound Boards to match ending sounds
/p/	pig, pepper	Lilly's Purple Plastic Purse, Mrs. Wishy-Washy, Who's In The Shed?, Three Little Pigs, The Snowy Day	Who's In The Shed?, Brown Bear
/r/	rose, write, rhythm	Jack's Garden, Paper Bag Princess, Wheels On The Bus	Who's In The Shed?, Brown Bear, Cookie's Week, Very Hungry Caterpillar, The Snowy Day
/s/	sit, scene, floss, city	Lilly's Purple Plastic Purse, Jack's Garden, If You Give A Mouse, Three Little Pigs, Yoko, The Snowy Day	Lilly's Purple Plastic Purse, Who's In The Shed?, I Know An Old Lady, Animals Should Definitely Not, If You Give A Mouse, Ten Black Dots, Bread and Jam for Frances, Mary Wore Her Red Dress, Where The Wild Things Are, Ten Black Dots
/t/	tie, slipped, kettle	Lilly's Purple Plastic Purse, Five Little Monkeys, Cookie's Week, Ten Black Dots	Jack's Garden, I Know An Old Lady, Cookie's Week, Wheels On The Bus, Curious George, Ten Black Dots, The Snowy Day, Mary Wore Her Red Dress
/v/	van, dove, of	Miss Nelson is Missing, Yoko	Five Little Monkeys, Paper Bag Princess
/w/	water, where, one	Mrs. Wishy-Washy, Very Hungry Caterpillar, Animals Should Definitely Not, Three Little Pigs	
/y/	you, few, use, feud	Yoko	
/z/	jazz, please, Xerox™, zoo	Five Little Monkeys	Very Hungry Caterpillar, Where the Wild Things Are, Corduroy
digraphs			
/sh/	shoe, sugar, lotion, issue	Who's In The Shed?, Brown Bear, Miss Nelson is Missing, Wheels On The Bus, Mary Wore Her Red Dress	Brown Bear
/sh/ (voiced)	pleasure, confusion		
/ch/	children, catch, future	Very Hungry Caterpillar, The Napping House	
/th/	think, breath	Five Little Monkeys	Paper Bag Princess
/th/ (voiced)	then, breathe,		
/ng/	thing, blink, English		Where The Wild Things Are
blends			
dr	drawer, dress, dragon	Cookie's Week, Paper Bag Princess, Mary Wore Her Red Dress	

Phoneme Vowels	as in...	Sound Boards to match beginning or medial sounds	Sound Boards to match ending sounds
a (long)	take, wait, hay, break, they	Jack's Garden, Paper Bag Princess, Yoko, Ten Black Dots, The Snowy Day	
a (short)	rat	Lilly's Purple Plastic Purse, Jack's Garden, Very Hungry Caterpillar, Paper Bag Princess, If You Give A Mouse, Wheels On The Bus, Where The Wild Things Are, The Napping House, Curious George, Yoko, Bread and Jam for Frances, Mary Wore Her Red Dress, Animals Should Definitely Not	
e (long)	eat, seed, equal, ski, receive	Lilly's Purple Plastic Purse, Jack's Garden, Five Little Monkeys, Who's In The Shed?, Brown Bear, Paper Bag Princess, Very Hungry Caterpillar, The Napping House, The Snowy Day, Mary Wore Her Red Dress	Lilly's Purple Plastic Purse, Mrs. Wishy-Washy, Five Little Monkeys, If You Give A Mouse, Yoko, Very Hungry Caterpillar
e (short)	egg, said, leopard, heifer, hen	Miss Nelson Is Missing, The Napping House, Bread and Jam for Frances, Mary Wore Her Red Dress, Animals Should Definitely Not	
i (long)	ice, rice, pie, light, my, buy	Five Little Monkeys, Miss Nelson Is Missing, Where The Wild Things Are, The Napping House, Curioous George	Where The Wild Things Are
i (short)	lit, build, symbol, pillage	Lilly's Purple Plastic Purse, Mrs. Wishy-Washy, Who's In The Shed?, Three Little Pigs, The Snowy Day	
o (long)	old, blow, foe, boat, though, sew	I Know An Old Lady, Miss Nelson Is Missing, Corduroy, Yoko	Five Little Monkeys, Yoko
o (short)	rot, water, autumn, law	I Know An Old Lady, Ten Black Dots	
u (long)	true, fued, grew, youth, through	Yoko, The Snowy Day	
u (short)	uncle, bug, umbrella, flood, some	Mrs. Wishy-Washy, Wheels On The Bus, Corduroy	
ur/ir	purse, bird, mother, giraffe	Lilly's Purple Plastic Purse, I Know An Old Lady, Corduroy, Mary Wore Her Red Dress, Animals Should Definitely Not, Brown Bear	Brown Bear

Phoneme Vowels	as in...	Sound Boards to match beginning sounds	Sound Boards to match ending sounds
or	horse, drawer	Who's In The Shed?, I Know An Old Lady, Cookie's Week, Curious George, Corduroy	
ar	garbage, car	Cookie's Week, Miss Nelson Is Missing	
ow	cow, sprout	Mrs. Wishy-Washy, Jack's Garden, Who's In The Shed?, If You Give A Mouse, Wheels On The Bus	Mrs. Wishy-Washy, Who's In The Shed?
aw	Washy, claw, walrus, autumn	Mrs. Wishy-Washy, Paper Bag Princess, Very Hungry Caterpillar, If You Give A Mouse, Where The Wild Things Are, Three Little Pigs, Animals Should Definitely Not	
oo/ew	two	Five Little Monkeys	Five Little Monkeys, Animals Should Definitely Not
oo	cookie, book, wolf	Cookie's Week, If You Give A Mouse, Three Little Pigs	
oy	toilet, boy	Cookie's Week	Corduroy

Chunks	or rhyming ... as in	Sound Boards to match rhyming sounds
A		
at	cat	Curious George, Mary Wore Her Red Dress
an	man	Curious George
ack	snack, Jack	Lilly's Purple Plastic Purse, Jack's Garden, Wheels On The Bus
ain	rain	Jack's Garden, Ten Black Dots
air/are	flair, bear, stare	Brown Bear
age	garbage	Cookie's Week
ave	cave	Paper Bag Princess
ark	shark	Miss Nelson Is Missing
aw	straw	If You Give A Mouse, Where The Wild Things Are, Three Little Pigs
all	ball	Corduroy
ax	Max, sacks	Where The Wild Things Are
ank	bank	Yoko
ace	lace, vase	Ten Black Dots
am	jam, lamb	Bread and Jam for Frances

Chunks	or rhyming ... as in	Sound Boards to match rhyming sounds
E		
ee/y	Lilly, three, baby	Lilly's Purple Plastic Purse, Mrs. Wishy-Washy, Five Little Monkeys, Cookie's Week, If You Give A Mouse, The Napping House, Yoko
en	hen	Animals Should Definitely Not
ed	bed, bread	The Napping House, Bread and Jam for Frances
er	teacher, mother	Lilly's Purple Plastic Purse, Brown Bear, Very Hungry Caterpillar, The Snowy Day
eed	seed	Jack's Garden
ew/oo	few, two, kangaroo	Five Little Monkeys, Animals Should Definitely Not
eep	sheep	Who's In The Shed?, Brown Bear
et	pet, toilet	Cookie's Week
eth	Elizabeth	Paper Bag Princess
erk	jerk, homework	Miss Nelson Is Missing
eeze	freeze, cheese	Very Hungry Caterpillar
ell/el	bell, angel	The Snowy Day
een/ean	green, jeans	Mary Wore Her Red Dress
ess	dress, Frances	Bread and Jam for Frances, Mary Wore Her Red Dress
eg	leg, egg	Bread and Jam for Frances
I		
ig	pig	Mrs. Wishy-Washy, Who's In The Shed?, Three Little Pigs
ing	king	Where The Wild Things Are
ive	five	Five Little Monkeys
irt	dirt	Mary Wore Her Red Dress
ird	bird	I Know An Old Lady
ish	fish	Brown Bear
in	napkin	If You Give A Mouse
ike	bike	Curious George
ild	child	The Napping House
irl	girl	Corduroy
ick	brick	Three Little Pigs, The Snowy Day
O		
ot	dot	Ten Black Dots
ow	cow	Mrs. Wishy-Washy, Who's In The Shed?
out	sprout	Jack's Garden
o	sprout	Five Little Monkeys, Yoko
or	for, drawer	Cookie's Week
orse	horse	Who's In The Shed?, I Know An Old Lady
oat	goat	I Know An Old Lady

Chunks	or rhyming ... as in	Sound Boards to match rhyming sounds
og	dog	I Know An Old Lady
ouse	mouse	If You Give A Mouse
ound	round	Wheels On The Bus
own	down	Wheels On The Bus
oy	boy	Corduroy
on	dragon, fun	Paper Bag Princess, Miss Nelson Is Missing, Very Hungry Caterpillar, Corduroy
ox	fox	Ten Black Dots
oot	boot, fruit	The Snowy Day
U		
uck	duck	Mrs. Wishy-Washy
urse	purse	Lilly's Purple Plastic Purse
us	walrus	Animals Should Definitely Not
un	fun, dragon	Paper Bag Princess, Miss Nelson Is Missing, Very Hungry Caterpillar, Corduroy
ull	pull, apple	Very Hungry Caterpillar
ut	shut	Wheels On The Bus
Y		
y	my, eye, cry	Where The Wild Things Are
y/ee	baby	Lilly's Purple Plastic Purse, Mrs. Wishy-Washy, Five Little Monkeys, Cookie's Week, If You Give A Mouse, The Napping House, Yoko

References

Adams, M. J. (1990). *Beginning to Read: Thinking and Learning about Print.* Cambridge, MA: MIT Press.

Adams, M. J., Foorman, B. R., Lundberg, I., & Beeler, T. (1998). *Phonemic Awareness In Young Children.* Baltimore: Paul H. Brookes Publishing Co.

Burns, S.M., Griffin, P., & Snow, C.E. (Eds., 1999). *Starting out Right: A Guide to Promoting Children's Reading Success.* Washington, DC: National Academy Press.

Blevins, W. (1998). *Phonics from A to Z: A Practical Guide.* New York: Scholastic.

Cassidy, J. & Cassidy, D (2000/2001)."What's Hot, What's Not for 2001." *Reading Today* 18 (3).

Cole, G. (2000). *Misreading Reading: The Bad Science That Hurts Children.* Portsmouth, NH: Heinemann.

Elkonin, D.B. (1973). "Methods of teaching reading: USSR". In J. Downing (Ed.), *Comparative Reading: Cross-national Studies of Behavior and Process in Reading and Writing* (pp. 551-580). New York: Macmillian.

Fitzpatrick, J. (1997). *Phonemic Awareness: Playing with Sounds to Strengthen Beginning Reading Skills.* Cypress, CA: Creative Teaching Press.

Honig. B. (1996). *Teaching Our Children to Read: the Role of Skills in a Comprehensive Reading Program.* Thousand Oaks, CA: Corwin Press.

International Reading Association, 1998. "Phonemic awareness and the teaching of reading: A position statement." Newark, DE: International Reading Association.

Juel, C., Griffith, P., & Gough, P. (1986). "Acquisition of Literacy: a Longitudinal Study of Children in First and Second Grade." *Journal of Educational Psychology*, 80.

Lyon, G. R. (1996). " Why Johnny can't decode." *The Washington Post*, 27 October.

Lyon, G.R. (1997). "Report on Learning Disabilities Research. Testimony Given to the Committee on Education and the Workforce, U.S. House of Representatives." Washington, DC

Routman, R. (2000). *Conversations: Strategies for Teaching, Learning, and Evaluating.* Portsmouth, NH: Heinemann.

Sensenbaugh, R. (1996). "Phonemic Awareness: An Important Early Step in Learning to Read." *ERIC Clearinghouse on Reading, English, and Communication Digest #19.*

Snow, C. E., Burns, M. S., & Griffin, P. (Eds., 1998). *Preventing Reading Difficulties in Young Children.* Washington, DC: National Academy Press.

Strickland, D. S. (1998). *Teaching Phonics Today: A Primer for Educators.* Newark, DE: International Reading Association.

Wagstaff, J. M. (1994). *Phonics That Work: New Strategies for the Reading/writing Classroom.* New York: Scholastic, Inc.

Wagstaff, J. M. & Sinatra, G. M. (1995). "Promoting Efficient and Independent Word Recognition: A New Strategy for Readers and Writers." *Balanced Reading Instruction.* 2, 27-37.

Wagstaff, J. M. (1997). "Building Practical Knowledge of Letter-Sound Correspondences: A Beginner's Word Wall and Beyond." *The Reading Teacher,* 51, 298-304.

Wagstaff, J. M. (1999). *Teaching reading and writing with word walls: Easy lessons and fresh ideas for creating interactive word walls that build literacy skills.* New York: Scholastic, Inc.

Yopp, H. K. (1992). "Developing phonemic awareness in young children." *The Reading Teacher,* 45, 696-703.

Appendix A

Phonemic Awareness

This book provides many ways to use sound boards to meet students' phonemic awareness needs. However, in order to use the boards most productively and creatively, it's important to have adequate background knowledge about phonemic awareness and how it relates to reading and writing development. The following questions and answers explore the difference between phonics and phonemic awareness and clarify why phonemic awareness is so important.

What's the difference between phonemic awareness and phonics?

The following simplified definitions can serve to help distinguish between phonemic awareness and phonics. Use them as references to complete the reader exercise below.

PHONICS	PHONEMIC AWARENESS
The relationship between sounds in speech and letters or groups of letters (spelling patterns).	Awareness of sounds within spoken words (apart from word meaning).
Spelling–sound correspondences	Ability to "hear," produce, and manipulate sounds.
For example: /g/ in goat /sh/ in ship /i – e/ in fine /eep/ in sleeping	For example: blending: /m/ + /a/ + /t/ = mat and segmenting: mat has three sounds /m/ /a/ /t/
PHONICS IS RELATED TO PRINT.	PHONEMIC AWARENESS IS RELATED TO ORAL AND AUDITORY PROCESSING.

Note: In precise terms, **phonological** awareness refers to knowledge of sound units in words at various levels including syllables, onsets and rimes, and phonemes. **Phonemic** awareness refers to work with sounds in words at the most discrete level: the phoneme level. Each term is widely used and often interchanged (Sensenbaugh, 1996).

Why Do I Need to Understand Phonemic Awareness?

As I share ideas about phonemic awareness with others, I use the *Phonemic Awareness? Phonics? or Both?* exercise that follows to bring home the importance of the topic. Please take a few moments to complete the exercise, read the discussion, and reflect on what it means for your teaching.

PHONEMIC AWARENESS? PHONICS? or BOTH?

Decide whether each of the activities should be categorized as phonemic awareness, phonics, or both and put a check mark in the appropriate column.

Activities	Phonemic Awareness	Phonics	Both
1. Making the word *stop* with magnetic letters, then generating *drop* and *pop* on the magnet board.			
2. Telling your neighbor three words that begin like *juice*.			
3. Identifying (circling, framing, or other) the words that begin like *three* in the shared reading of a poem.			
4. Reciting classic nursery rhymes.			
5. Repeating *Baa, Baa, Black Sheep* and practicing the formation of the letter *b*.			
6. Singing *Jack and Jill*, changing initial sounds to say /ch/. (*Chack and Chill went up the chill to chetch a pail of chater...*)			
7. Making a store of /s/ words. Children help write the list through "sharing the pen" (interactive writing).			
8. Hunting for words beginning with /sh/ to write on index cards.			
9. Sorting index cards for words with *at, ot,* and *ip*.			
10. Before chanting the rhyme *Miss Mary Mack*, the teacher asks children to listen for the /m/ words. After each line, the class repeats the /m/ words.			
11. Using temporary spelling during writing workshop.			
12. Adding *Rr* words to alphabet books.			
13. Students push M&M's™ into sound boxes as they hear the sounds in words like *pin, sat,* and *jog*.			

Discussion of the Reader Exercise

Phonemic awareness and phonics are not the same but are mutually dependent (Fitzpatrick, 1997).

Strictly phonemic-awareness activities = 2, 4, 6, 10, 13. All of these involve oral language play only—sounds, not letters. Numbers 2 and 10 involve sound matching—distinguishing a beginning sound and generating or recognizing other like-sounding words. Number 4 involves tuning the ability to hear rhyme. Number 6 involves phoneme substitution—substituting beginning sounds with a target sound. In activity 13, students are segmenting words into sound units (either onset and rime */p/ /in/*) and/or phonemes *(/p/ /i/ /n/)* .

Phonics only activities = 3, 8, 9, 12. All of these activities involve print. And, arguably, they could all be completed without knowledge of sound.

With number 3, students could search the poem for words that begin with the same visual features or letters (th) as other identified words without having any clue what sound /th/ makes and without understanding how the words sound alike. Numbers 8 and 12 could be completed the same way. Rather than listening for or generating words that begin with the /sh/ or /r/ sounds, children could rely solely on matching visual features. Words from around the room that look like they begin with the matching letters *sh* and *r* could be written on index cards or added to alphabet books. Words that look the same, ending with *at, ot,* and *ip,* could be sorted visually into piles to complete activity 9. In fact, students with low phonemic awareness sometimes compensate with these kinds of letter-matching strategies.

Activities that depend on both = 3, 8, 9, 12. Yes, these are the same as the phonics-only activities. But, as you consider each one, ask yourself, what is the true nature of this instructional activity? What do I want kids to do here? In answering these simple questions, it is clear that **all phonics activities have a phonemic awareness component.** For these activities we want students to hear, recognize, produce, and match the target **sounds** in addition to associating them with **letters.** The ability to work with sounds is at the core. If we find students relying solely on how the words *look*, we have to say, "Now wait a minute. Listen to this sound…"

So, all the activities in the exercise, with the exception of numbers 2, 4, 6, 10, and 13, which lack a print component, can rightfully be characterized as **both** phonemic awareness and phonics.

As the reader exercise illustrates, it is vitally important that students have phonemic awareness skills if we expect them to use letter–sound correspondences and phonics strategies as developing readers and writers. Thus it is critical for us to understand phonemic awareness and what its implications are in the classroom. All of our phonics lessons depend on it.

In sum, all we hope our students will learn about letters and sounds during our reading and writing demonstrations and focused mini-lessons depends on their phonemic awareness. Do they understand that words are made up of sounds? How sophisticated are their understandings? Can they blend sounds to make words? Can they segment words into sounds? How proficiently? If they are unable to accomplish these tasks orally, how will they accomplish them when letters are involved?

> *It is critical that teachers are familiar with the concept of phonemic awareness and that they know that there is a body of evidence pointing to a significant relation between phonemic awareness and reading acquisition. This cannot be ignored.*
>
> *International Reading Association, 1998.*

> *Visual word recognition can flourish only when children displace the belief that print is like pictures with the insight that written words are comprised of letters that, in turn, map to speech sounds.*
>
> *Snow, Burns, and Griffin, 1998, p. 45*

> *It is unlikely that children lacking phonemic awareness can benefit fully from phonics instruction since they do not understand what letters and spellings are supposed to represent.*
>
> *Juel, Griffith, & Gough, 1986*

What Phonemic-Awareness Skills Do Students Need—and When?

As teachers learn about the importance of phonemic awareness, they often ask, "What is expected for students at my grade level?" I researched this question and found the following general expectations for students as they finish kindergarten, first, and second grades. Remember these are generalities. Goals for your students should be based on assessments of their unique abilities.

> *Phonics, in short, presumes a working awareness of the phonemic composition of words. In conventional phonics programs, however, such awareness was generally taken for granted, and therein lies the force of the research on phonemic awareness. To the extent that children lack such phonemic awareness, they are unable usefully to internalize their phonics lessons.*
>
> *Snow, Burns, and Griffin, 1998, p. 55*

General Expectations:
Phonemic Awareness (and related Phonics Skills)

Kindergartners

❖ can hear separate words in sentences.

❖ can hear syllables in words.

❖ can match like sounds in words at beginning and end
(e.g., *book* sounds like *boat).*

❖ can recognize rhyming words.

Strickland (1998)

❖ given spoken segments, can merge them into target word
(e.g., *car + pet = carpet*).

❖ given a spoken word, can produce a rhyming word.

❖ can understand that the sequence of letters in a written word
corresponds to the sequence of sounds in a spoken word.

❖ can use phonemic awareness and letter knowledge to spell
independently.

Snow, Burns, & Griffin (Eds., 1998)

First Graders

❖ can match similar medial sounds in short words
(e.g., *pig* sounds like *fit*).

❖ can segment and blend phonemes in short words
(e.g., *pig* = /p/ /i/ /g/ or /p/+/i/+/g/= *pig*).

❖ can use patterns in known words (onset–rime analogies)
to identify unknown words (e.g. if I know *cat,* this is *flat).*

Strickland (1998)

❖ can count the number of syllables in a word.

❖ can blend or segment phonemes of most one-syllable words.

❖ can use invented spelling to spell independently.

Snow, Burns, & Griffin (Eds., 1998)

Second Graders

❖ have increasing ability to segment words for phonics/spelling (e.g., I hear /sh//i//p//m//ent/ in the word *shipment*).

❖ have increasing ability to use patterns in known words (onset–rime analogies) to identify unknown words (e.g., If I know *rip* and *pick*, this is *lipstick*).

Strickland (1998)

❖ can represent the complete sound of a word when spelling independently (includes vowel in every syllable).

❖ can correctly represent spelling patterns in his or her writing.

Snow, Burns, & Griffin (Eds., 1998)

Sources:

Strickland, D. S. (1998). *Teaching Phonics Today: A Primer for Educators.* Newark, DE: International Reading Association.

Snow, C. E., Burns, M. S., and Griffin, P. (Eds., 1998). *Preventing Reading Difficulties in Young Children.* Washington, DC: National Academy Press.

And republished in:

Burns, S.M., Griffin, P., and Snow, C.E. (1999). *Starting Out Right: A Guide to Promoting Children's Reading Success.* Washington, DC: National Academy Press.

Appendix B

Levels of Phonemic Awareness (Adams, 1990)

The following levels proceed from easiest to most difficult. For example, children who can hear rhyming words (level I) but cannot discriminate between beginning sounds (level II) will benefit less from phonics instruction than those who can. Likewise, children who can blend syllables together (level III) to make words but cannot blend onsets and rimes (also level III) to make words have less sophisticated word knowledge than those who can.

I. The ability to hear rhyme and alliteration.

Can the child distinguish rhyming words from non-rhyming words?

II. The ability to discriminate between sounds.

Can the child distinguish between words that begin the same onset, end with the same rime, and end with the same sound (phoneme level)? Essentially, the child will be matching words that go together on different levels of complexity.

III. The ability to blend sounds and split syllables.

Can the child blend syllables, onsets and rimes, and phonemes? Can the child split words into syllables?

IV. The ability to segment sounds.

Can the child divide words into sound segments at the syllable level, onset and rime level, and phoneme level? It is useful to provide the child with manipulatives (blocks, chips, etc.) to represent the sound segments.

V. The ability to manipulate (add, delete, or substitute) sounds.

Can the child add, delete, or substitute sound segments in words at the syllable level, onset and rime level, and phoneme level?

Phonemic-Awareness Assessments

The assessment items below match Adams' *Levels of Phonemic Awareness*. They are set up from easiest to hardest. Since it is easier for students to deal with larger units (syllables) than smaller units (onsets and rimes, phonemes), each assessment item is set up accordingly. When using each assessment item, do a few examples with the student first to be sure he or she understands the directions. Remember these tasks are done orally—no print is involved.

I. The ability to hear rhyme and alliteration.

Can the child distinguish rhyming words from non-rhyming words?

Assessment

Recite *I'm A Little Teapot* and *Itsy Bitsy Spider*. Emphasize the words that rhyme with *out*, saying them slowly and explaining that these words have the same ending sounds—they rhyme. Ask the children to listen to these words and clap if the words rhyme (or tell you *yes* or *no*).

out/spout	short/out	stout/out	up/out
shout/out	rain/out	spider/out	

II. The ability to discriminate between sounds.

Can the child distinguish between words that begin the same onset, end with the same rime, and end with the same sound (phoneme level)? Essentially, the child will be matching words that go together on different levels of complexity.

Assessment

Which two of these words begin with the same sound?

tap/tug/hit	rain/rug/apple
pot/song/pipe	fire/cloud/food

Which of these words end with the same sound? (rime level)

hit/split/wear	cake/train/snake
fun/sun/tap	trip/fish/whip

Which of these words end with the same sound? (phoneme level)

hop/camp/sand	wish/tan/bun
track/bike/wrap	hunt/run/bat

III. The ability to blend sounds and split syllables.

Can the child blend syllables, onsets and rimes, and phonemes? Can the child split words into syllables?

Blending Assessment

I'm going to say some words slowly by stretching them into parts. Listen to the parts and put them back together. (syllable level)

cow	boy	sun	shine
win	dow	pen	oil

I'm going to say some words slowly by stretching them into parts. Listen to the parts and put them back together. (onset and rime level)

        c   an   n   ight

        dr ess   str ike

I'm going to say some words slowly by stretching them into parts. Listen to the parts and put them back together. (phoneme level)

      /p/ /a/ /t/   /w/ /a/ /sh/

      /j/ /u/ /m/ /p/   /s/ /m/ /e/ /l/

Splitting Assessment

I'm going to say some words. Clap to show how many parts you hear in each word. (syllable level)

        sink (1)   tonight (2)

        dinner (2)   butterfly (3)

IV. The ability to segment sounds.

Can the child divide words into sound segments at the syllable level, onset and rime level, and phoneme level? It is useful to provide the child with manipulatives (blocks, chips, etc.) to represent the sound segments.

Assess

I'm going to say some words. Tell me the parts you hear. (syllable level)

      bedroom /bed/ /room/   sometimes /some/ /times/

      finger /fing/ /er/   chattering /chat/ /ter/ /ing/

I'm going to say some words. Tell me the sounds you hear. (onset and rime level)

      tap /t/ /ap/   thin /th/ /in/

      stamp /st/ /amp/   block /bl/ /ock/

I'm going to say some words. Say the words slowly and tell me every sound you hear. (phoneme level)

        pan /p/ /a/ /n/   tape /t/ /a/ /p/

        went /w/ /e/ /n/ /t/ smart /s/ /m/ /ar/ /t/

V. The ability to manipulate (add, delete, or substitute) sounds. Can the child add, delete, or substitute sound segments in words at the syllable level, onset and rime level, and phoneme level?

Deletion Assessment

Say *campsite* without the *camp*.	(syllable level)
Say *running* without the *ing*.	(syllable level)
Say *beat* without the /b/.	(onset and rime level)
Say *crunch* without the *unch*.	(onset and rime level)
Say *bunt* without the /t/.	(phoneme level)
Say *trick* without the /t/.	(phoneme level)

Substitution Assessment

Say *classroom* with *ball* at the beginning.	(syllable level)
Say *trick* with /t/ at the beginning.	(onset and rime level)
Say *hot* with /p/ at the end.	(phoneme level)
Say *beach* with /t/ at the end.	(phoneme level)

Resources for Phonemic-Awareness Assessment

Group Assessment Tool:

Adams, M. J., Foorman, B. R., Lundberg, I., & Beeler, T. (1998). *Phonemic Awareness In Young Children.* Baltimore: Paul H. Brookes Publishing Co. (Chapter 10) (www.pbrookes.com)

Individual Assessment Tools:

Blevins, W. (1998). *Phonics from A to Z: A Practical Guide.* New York: Scholastic. (p. 31) (1-800-325-6149)

Robertson, C. & Salter, W. (1997). "The Phonological Awareness Test." East Moline, IL: LinguiSystems, Inc. (1-800-776-4332)

Torgesen, J. K. & Bryant, B. (1994). *Phonological Awareness Training for Reading.* Austin, TX: PRO-ED.

Yopp, H.K. (1995). A test for assessing phonemic awareness in young children. *The Reading Teacher*, 49(1), 20-29.

Family Letter A letter to send home with your students

Dear Families,

Phonemic awareness may be an intimidating term, but it is an important one for us to understand as we work with our youngsters.

Why is it important? Phonemic awareness has been found to be the single most powerful predictor of whether or not children will learn to read successfully.

So, what is it? Phonemic awareness is the awareness of sounds in words. Knowing that words are made up of sounds, hearing sounds in words, blending sounds together to make words, and breaking words apart into sounds are all forms of phonemic awareness. The more our children are aware of how sounds work in oral language, the better readers and writers they will be.

What can we do about it? It's simple to promote phonemic awareness with your child by playing sound games as suggested below. There is no paper or pencil involved, just oral interaction between you and your child. These games can be played anytime, anywhere. And, kids love them!

To work on:

Rhyming words

You say: "I'll say a word like *pan,* and you give me a rhyming word like *tan.*" Give your child several words to rhyme, then allow him or her to give you words to rhyme.

Words with the same beginning sound:

You say: "I'll give you a word like *stop* and you give me a word that starts with the same sound—like *stain.*" Give your child several words to match, then allow him or her to give you words to match.

Words with the same ending sound:

You say: "I'll give you a word like *pig* and you give me a word that ends with the same sound—like *tag.*" Give your child several words to match, then allow him or her to give you words to match.

Clapping the syllables in words:

You say: "Let's clap these word parts: hel/i/cop/ter; shop/ping; can/dy. Let's try some more."

Putting sounds together to make words:

You say: "Let's put these sounds together to make a word: /t/ /a/ /p/...tap. Let's try another."

Counting the sounds in words:

You say, "How many sounds do you hear in the word *kid?* (/k/ /i/ /d/...three sounds). Let's try another."

Breaking words apart into sounds:

You say: "What sounds do you hear in *red*? (/r/ /e/ /d/). Let's try another."

When you're playing these oral word games with your child, give lots of examples. If he or she has trouble, say the words or sounds together and repeat them several times. After practice, your child should be able to pick up on rhyming words, hearing and comparing beginning and ending sounds, putting sounds together to make words, and breaking words apart into sounds. Remember to have fun! If your child grows tired, stop. You can always pick up again later while driving in the car, waiting in line at the supermarket, taking a walk, setting the table for dinner, getting dressed for school…

Volunteers' Instructions for Using Sound Boards

Matching Beginning Sounds

Dear Volunteer,

Thanks for helping! You are invaluable to the success of our program.

Here are some instructions for using the attached activity sheet (sound board).

1. *Have students identify the pictures. Say them together.*

2. *Give each student a handful of edible markers (from the attached bag). Tell students they will mark their board under the picture **that begins with the same sound** as the words you say.*

3. *Say a word that begins with the same sound as one of the pictures. For example, if Sammi is pictured, say sausage.*

4. *Have students repeat the word to match (sausage).*

5. *Have students test each column to see which picture begins with the same sound as the given word (sausage). (They may say something like: "Joe—sausage, no that doesn't start the same. Sammi—sausage, yes that starts the same!")*

6. *Ask students to place a marker in the column with the picture that matches.*

7. *Continue saying words that begin with the sounds of the items pictured. Students should always repeat the words you give and test the columns before placing a marker on the board.*

8. *When time is up, allow students to eat their markers. Collect the sound boards.*

Matching Rhyming Words

Dear Volunteer,

Thanks for helping! You are invaluable to the success of our program.

Here are some instructions for using the attached activity sheet (sound board).

1. *Have students identify the pictures. Say them together.*

2. *Give each student a handful of edible markers (from the attached bag). Tell students they will mark their board under the picture **that rhymes** with the words you say.*

3. *Say a word that rhymes with one of the pictures. For example, if a pig is pictured, say big.*

4. Have students repeat the word to match (big).

5. Have students test each column to see which picture rhymes with the given word (in this case big). (They may say something like: "Cow—big, no those don't rhyme. Pig—big, yes those rhyme!")

6. Ask students to place a marker in the column with the picture that rhymes.

7. Continue saying words that rhyme with the items pictured. Students should always repeat the words you give and test the columns before placing a marker on the board.

8. When time is up, allow students to eat their markers. Collect the sound boards.

Matching Ending Sounds

Dear Volunteer,

Thanks for helping! You are invaluable to the success of our program.

Here are some instructions for using the attached activity sheet (sound board).

1. Have students identify the pictures. Say them together.

2. Give each student a handful of edible markers (from the attached bag). Tell students they will mark their board under the picture **that ends with the same sound** as the words you say.

3. Say a word that ends with the same sound as one of the pictures. For example, if a horse is pictured, say kiss.

4. Have students repeat the word to match (kiss).

5. Have students test each column to see which picture ends with the same sound as the given word (kiss). (They may say something like: "Cow—kiss, no those don't end the same. Horse—kiss, yes those end with the same sound!")

6. Ask students to place a marker in the column with the picture that matches.

7. Continue saying words that end with the sounds of the items pictured. Students should always repeat the words you give and test the columns before placing a marker on the board.

8. When time is up, allow students to eat their markers. Collect the sound boards.

Matching Vowel Sounds:

Dear Volunteer,

Thanks for helping! You are invaluable to the success of our program.

Here are some instructions for using the attached activity sheet (sound board).

1. *Have students identify the pictures. Say them together.*

2. *Give each student a handful of manipulatives (from the attached bag). Tell students they will mark their board under the picture **that has the same vowel sound** as the words you say.*

3. *Say a word that has the same vowel sound as one of the pictures. For example, if a bike is pictured, say* light.

4. *Have students repeat the word to match (*light*).*

5. *Have students test each column to see which picture has the same vowel sound as the given word (*light*). (They may say something like: "book— light, no those don't have the same vowel sound. Bike—light, yes those have the same vowel sound!")*

6. *Ask students to place a marker in the column with the picture that matches.*

7. *Continue saying words that have the same vowel sounds as the items pictured. Students should always repeat the words you give and test the columns before placing a marker on the board.*

8. *When time is up, allow students to eat their markers. Collect the sound boards.*

Notes

Notes